CATHERINA McKIERNAN
Running for my life

Ian O'Riordan

With a foreword by
Paula Radcliffe

Red Rock Press

CATHERINA McKIERNAN
Running for my life

First published 2005

Red Rock Press
www.redrockpress.ie

Glengyle
Claremont Road
Howth
Dublin 13
Ireland

redrockpress@eircom.net

This edition published 2005

ISBN 0-9548653-1-6

Editing and design: **Stephen Ryan**
Copy editing: **Richard Gallagher**
Printing: **GraficasCems** (Spain)
Printing liaison: **Hugh Stancliffe**
Photographs: **Sportsfile** except where otherwise credited.
Index: **Mark Gilleece**
www.redrockpress.ie

Acknowledgements

This book is dedicated to my parents, John and Kathleen,
for their support and encouragement,
my husband Damien and daughter Deirbhile,
my family, friends and supporters.

To the late Brian Johnston.

To my agent Ray Flynn.

To Joe Doonan for his years of great coaching, mentoring and advice.

To Phil Brady and Brady's garages, Brendan and Eugene Murtagh in
Kingspan, Cornafean GFC, Ballyhaise GFC, Ramor Utd GFC,
Boxmore Plastics, Kiernan Milling, Sean Quinn and the Slieve Russell
Hotel Ballyconnell, Jackson's garages in Cavan, County Cavan golf club, and
the Cavan GAA county board and all of the other individuals and businesses
who supported me during my years on the circuit.

To Paul and Lucy Maloney and adidas in Ireland and the UK.

To Frank Greally, Brian Carthy, David Markey,
Don O'Mahony and Paul O'Grady

And finally to all the athletes whom I have competed against and
run with, and to all athletics fans everywhere,
thank you for a most wonderful run in life.

IMPOSSIBLE IS NOTHING

Life on the run

November 30th: 1969 Born Drumkeerin, Cornafean, Cavan.

March 1988: Wins Irish Schools senior cross country title.

March 1989: Runs her first World Cross Country champions in Stavanger, Norway, and finished in 76th position.

February 1990: Wins her first National Senior Cross Country title.

July 1990: Wins her first National Senior track title over 3,000 metres.

March 1992: Wins the silver medal behind Lynn Jennings at the World Cross Country championships in Boston.

August 1992: Runs the 3,000 metres at the Barcelona Olympics, finishes eighth in her 3,000 metres heat.

March 1993: Wins a second consecutive silver medal at the World Cross Country in Amorebiata, Spain.

March 1994: Wins a third consecutive silver medal at the World Cross Country in Budapest, Hungary.

December 1994: Wins gold at the first European Cross Country championships in Northumberland, England.

March 1994: Wins a fourth consecutive silver medal at the World Cross Country in Durham, England.

August 1996: Finishes in 11th place in the 10,000 metres final of the Atlanta Olympics.

September 1997: Wins the Berlin Marathon in 2:23.44, the fastest debut in women's marathon history.

April 1998: Wins the London Marathon in 2:26.26.

November 1998: Wins the Amsterdam Marathon in 2:22.23.

October 1999: 12th place in the Chicago Marathon in 2:35.51.

July 2000: Withdraws from the Sydney Olympic marathon because of injury.

March 2004: Returns to the World Cross Country in Brussels for the first time in seven years, and finishes in 30th position.

September 2004: Runs her last major race at the Great North Run in England, and finishes her career a month later by winning the Cavan 10km road race, retiring immediately afterwards.

FOREWORD
BY PAULA RADCLIFFE

Paul Radcliffe winning the Marathon at the 2005 World Athletics Championships in Helsinki

IT'S NOT A NORMAL THING FOR ME TO dream about other athletes the night before a big race. I normally sleep soundly before any race, but the night before I ran the London marathon in 2002 I had a dream about Catherina McKiernan.

I had watched Catherina win the race back in 1998, and her victory obviously made a lasting impression on me. I still can't quite figure out how or why she came into my mind, but I was obviously thinking about following on in her footsteps, and winning the London marathon for myself. It was very strange though, and the dream itself made no real sense. Catherina was showing me around her new house, which she was decorating herself. She wanted to take me into all the different rooms. Very strange, as I say, but I must have been thinking about running well the next day, and winning the race the same as Catherina had done.

FOREWORD

Maybe it was because I had known Catherina for such a long time. We first crossed paths 10 years earlier at the World Cross Country Championships in Boston in 1992. I don't remember actually meeting Catherina there, but I definitely remember how well she ran.

I had won the junior women's race earlier in the day. I'd finished with the medal ceremony and my warm-down before the senior women started, so I had a good chance to see most of that race. And I was very impressed with how Catherina ran that day.

In many ways it inspired me a little more to see the way she ran, and how close Catherina came to winning the gold medal. Even winning the silver medal was really impressive. She was young and yet determined and able to run with the best of them.

I also think Catherina showed me from the very beginning that you can compete with the Africans. Sometimes the European men don't believe you can compete with the Africans, but I've never believed that, and watching Catherina do it just reinforced that belief. I never saw any reason why I couldn't, especially when I saw people like Catherina go out there and take it right to them.

I do remember the first time I raced Catherina. It was at the Mallusk international race in Belfast a year later, when we were both building towards the World Cross Country in 1993. She beat me on the day, but I remember coming away very encouraged that I'd actually managed to get quite close to her.

From the very beginning Catherina was always very friendly to me and always very approachable. I know she does come across sometimes as being very shy to some people, but she was always willing to talk to me before or after a race.

Between the cross-country and the track races we would see each other at least a few times every year. In 1996 we also met up at the high-altitude training village of Font Romeu in the French Alps, where I had bought an apartment.

Catherina came up there to train with her coach, Joe Doonan. I remember Noel Berkeley was there too, another athlete working with Joe. Catherina was doing most of her runs on her own, which I think was the way Joe preferred it. Most days I would also go running above 1,900 metres, up on the plateau, but Joe didn't want her going up that high. That was too bad, because it is beautiful up there. So we only ended up training together a couple of times.

There was one time before a race in Spain when we had a good run together. But we did warm down together a bunch of times and would happily chat away about different stuff.

We did race against each other quite a few times in cross-country, but only a few times on the track, because we were mostly doing different events. Like when we were both at the Atlanta Olympics, and she was doing the 10,000 metres and I was doing the 5,000 metres.

But I do know Catherina ran some very good times on the track. I think it's unfair that some people still think she didn't really perform on the track. Part of that is the fact that she was such a good cross-country runner and was probably judged on that. That doesn't mean she wasn't a good track runner. She'll probably admit herself that she had a lot more success on the cross-country, winning four World Cross Country silver medals in succession. That meant she was probably a little tired going into the track season.

I think it was always inevitable that she would move up to the marathon, and when she made her debut in Berlin I was very impressed. I would have always said beforehand that Catherina would run a good marathon, and yet you never really know with the marathon, because there's so much that can go wrong running 26 miles. She just went straight in there and did it first time of asking. It was the fastest debut ever by a woman, and that definitely led the way forward for a while. She proved that anything was possible in your debut marathon, that you didn't need to learn about the distance and you didn't need to fear it. You just go in there and give it your best shot, and if everything works out you can run a fast time on your first attempt.

That did have an influence on me when I too moved up to the marathon. She came from a cross-country background similar to me and had made the move up very successfully. But the big influence was her mental approach. She got stuck into the distance in a really positive way, and it paid off. That's the way I wanted to run a marathon too.

I think it's easy to forget how determined Catherina was, because mentally she was very tough. People didn't always see that side of her. She always comes across as nice and a little shy, but she's always been a very tough competitor. She always showed that in cross-country and again when she moved up to the marathon. It was the same when she ran the London marathon in 1998.

I was watching that race on the television, and this time not everything went to plan. She had some very bad stomach problems towards the end of the race, but she was clearly very focused, and just didn't let it bother her. She just took it all in her stride and did what she had to do.

It takes a very tough competitor to do that, to carry on when things start going against you. I think the Catherina most people know off the track would have been very distraught by that, but her competitive nature just kept her focused.

It was amazing that both Catherina and Sonia O'Sullivan came along at the same time. You knew whenever you raced the Irish girls you were going to have to run hard, whether it was Catherina on the cross-country or Sonia on the track. And that's the way I would have wanted it. I always enjoyed the competition. Any time I lined up with Catherina I knew it was going to be a hard race from the gun, and that's the way I liked it. So I think my rivalry with her was always friendly. I was always glad to have Catherina in a race.

It was a shame though that she picked up a few injuries after the Amsterdam marathon in 1998 because I think she could have run a lot faster at the distance. She did manage to come back and run a few more cross-country and road races, but I can understand why she did only one more marathon. It is an event that takes a lot out of your body, and when you start having injury problems one after another and you just can't get over them it's very difficult to make it back to the top. That's always been my worst fear, that I'll have some injuries that I just can't get over.

So Catherina just got on with the rest of her life. She's happy now with a family and still loves her running as much as ever. That's about all any athlete can ask for. I recently met her again at an event to mark the 25th anniversary of the London marathon. I wasn't surprised at all to see she still looked plenty fit to run a marathon.

We chatted again like old times, and I could tell Catherina was quite proud to be part of the London Club, as they now call all the past winners. And she should be. She produced a great victory there in 1998. Winning the London marathon has been one of the highlights of my career, and Catherina can proudly count it as one of hers too.

Paula Radcliffe ran two hours, 15 minutes 25 seconds to win the London marathon in 2003. It remains the fastest women's marathon time ever run, almost three and a half minutes quicker than the next-best woman.

CHAPTER 1
THE TROUBLES I'VE SEEN

I WAS BORN TO RUN. SINCE I FIRST LEARNT TO TIE MY SHOELACES I could run as far as I wanted, and usually as fast as I wanted. There's hardly been one day in my life when I didn't want to run. I know running is not the most important thing in life. It's just that it was the most important thing in my life.

It's hard for me to explain why I love running so much. It's harder still to explain why I started to hate running so much. It was a love affair – the best of times and the worst of times.

The moment when that love of running ended was June 2000, about two months before the start of the Sydney Olympics. I didn't quite realise it at the time but I'd lost control over the one thing that mattered most in my life. I would spend the next four years trying to regain that control, trying to rediscover that love of running.

As far as everyone around me was concerned, I was going to Sydney to run the Olympic marathon. If everything went to plan I was going to win it – bring home the gold medal to Ireland. I had the ability to win and if I had the confidence to go with that then I was one of very few that could win.

In the three years before Sydney I had won major marathons in Berlin,

London and Amsterdam. When I won in Berlin I ran the fastest ever debut marathon by a woman. London is one of the top marathons in the world, and winning there automatically made me one of the world leaders in women's marathon running. When I won in Amsterdam I came close to breaking the world record on a day when a strong wind denied me a place in athletics history. During that time I had established myself as the world's best female marathon runner.

Yet in the months leading up to the Sydney Olympics the last thing in the world I wanted to do was run another marathon. The thought of running in Sydney was terrifying me. I'd go to bed thinking about it, and I'd wake up thinking about it. All day long it entered my every thought with a heavy sense of dread. When my husband, Damien O'Reilly, thinks back he figures it was the closest thing he'd seen to a breakdown. I don't know if I'd go that far but it was definitely the most frustrating and annoying period of my life.

Then, one evening in the middle of summer, I decided that I was not going to Sydney. Damien was there to witness the moment. So was my brother Peadar. They had both stood close by me over the previous year as crack after crack started to appear in the plan to win that Olympic gold medal. During that time I'd gone from being the best marathon runner in the world to someone who couldn't finish the simplest of training runs. But I knew that day in July that nobody in the world could persuade me to run in the Olympics. I had all but given up myself two months earlier, and now the last efforts of those around me were about to fail as well.

On the last Sunday in April 2000 I'd gone to the town of La Courneuve, near Paris, for a 15-kilometre road race. I'd won there twice and thought another victory would restore at least some of the confidence I needed to stay on course for a successful run in Sydney. My training had been progressing reasonably well since the end of February, even though the year itself had started out with the sort of setback I was suddenly becoming well used to.

Instead of running the Belfast International Cross Country on January 5th, my traditional start to another season, I was travelling to Limerick to see Ger Hartmann, probably the most sought-after sports-injury therapist in the country. I'd convinced myself he was going to provide the instant cure I so desperately craved. What I got instead was further desperation.

Ger recommended an MRI scan as part of the treatment, and that revealed a stress fracture to a small bone at the base of my left ankle. Six weeks off the road, I was told. Ger wanted to put me on a recovery programme. At first I agreed, but I couldn't commit to it; my heart just wasn't in it.

But just standing on the starting line in Paris I felt like I was taking a small step in the right direction. For the opening few kilometres the legs were just about holding up but I just wasn't feeling particularly good. Without warning, the pain started, nowhere specific, just bad enough to know this was going to be a lot more difficult than I'd hoped. By the halfway point I was several hundred yards down on the leaders and my race was over.

I crossed the finish line and glanced at the clock. Fifty-four minutes something. I could normally run 15 kilometres in just under 49 minutes. I had no idea where I finished until one of the race organisers came up to me.

Well done, he said, you were 12th. I tried to raise a smile. All I wanted to do was get to the airport and get back home as fast as I could.

No matter how I'd performed in either a race or a training session I would always make note of it in my diary. It's habit, one of the last things I do before going to bed. Like brushing my teeth.

Felt terrible, ran awful. 15km in 54 minutes. Initially that was all I could write. I needed to explain more than that. But I just didn't know what was wrong with me. I mean I just couldn't be that bad unless something was seriously wrong with me. Or could I?

The next day I went for my usual recovery run in the Phoenix Park. My mind was heavy with negative thoughts. Some newspaper reports that morning were making it sound like I was on my way back. She was able to run hard, and without pain, they said. If they only realised that wasn't the problem. My confidence was disintegrating. So was my desire to train hard.

If I had met someone in the Park and they told me there and then to forget about the Olympics, I would have shook their hand. Deal. I would have done a deal with the devil that day.

When I got home I rang my coach, Joe Doonan. No matter what happened with my running Joe was usually the first to hear about it. We'd been like teacher and student for over 10 years, but it was never easy for me to explain my races to him. It didn't matter whether I had good news or bad news, I just found it hard to get my thoughts across to him.

On that occasion it was particularly hard.

He didn't seem too annoyed about it, or at least didn't really want to dwell on it. That was always one of his coaching philosophies, not to dwell on it. We agreed to go into Trinity College and do a few tests on the treadmill, just to check the engine was still running smoothly. If a computer told me I was fit enough to run a certain time then I couldn't argue with that.

Bernard Donne had being doing these tests on me for several years now and was always good for a laugh. He's quite blunt. You could be feeling really down about something and Bernard could snap you out of it with just one sentence.

Yeah, you can still run all right, he said.

I raised a smile but I didn't snap out of it.

I'd first done a treadmill test about 10 years previously, to test my VO2 max. That meant nothing to me at the time, like being told the brake horsepower of a car. Essentially, a VO2 max test will tell you how efficiently the body uses oxygen. The greater the uptake of oxygen the greater the potential to run long distances. By the time I was leaving I remember Bernard was very excited about this skinny little girl from Cavan. I remember him saying it was the highest VO2 max he'd ever seen, and that meant some day I'd run a great marathon.

Leaving Trinity I was feeling a little better about myself. Bernard had convinced me that physically I was actually making quite good progress. The engine was still in good condition. It was up to me to improve things mentally.

Joe had a lot of time for Bernard and for Dr Mary Kelly, his partner in the Physiology Department at Trinity. Both of them have been innovative in working out problems with my training and preparation.

Physically then, everything appeared to be fine. For the first few weeks in May the training continued more or less uninterrupted. Most of the stuff I wrote in my diary was short and sweet, and that was generally a good sign.

The days were getting steadily warmer, and as the trees came into full bloom I could sometimes feel my body responding, as if the turning of the seasons was helping me turn the corner. Maybe there was still enough hunger left inside of me to make it to Sydney.

But towards the end of May I began to feel a pain in my lower back. It wasn't too specific, but a sort-of general numbness that seemed to spread into the top of my buttocks. On May 28th I wrote in my diary that I was running through pain. That's never a good sign.

My massage therapist Dave Corcoran did his best to ease the discomfort. Dave had shared many a 20-mile run with me around Malahide Castle, and from his own running background he knows that athletes reach a certain threshold after which they can no longer run through the pain of an injury. He figured I had crossed that point already.

For a couple of days my back was very tight. Every training run had become a real struggle, and most days had to be cut short. I'd leave the house feeling bad and come back feeling worse. Sometimes I'd just lie down in the middle of the sitting room, staring up at the ceiling, trying to make some sense of the situation. Every day I lost more heart. And most days I would wake up with absolutely no interest in, or desire to go, training. I felt like I'd forgotten how to run. I just couldn't put one foot in front of the other and stride out effortlessly the way I once could.

Everywhere I went people seemed to be asking me about the injuries. How's the back? How's the knee? How's the ankle? Ah grand, I'd say.

Good luck so, they'd say. As if luck had anything to do with it.

If they'd asked me about my desire to run maybe I would have told them the truth. It was gone.

I knew from the summers of 1997 and 1998 what level of training I needed to be at. I was flying then, every run and every session creating a real buzz, that blissful high that you know can be created only with a rush of natural endorphins. I knew what it was like to be training well, where every session would seem to bring about some improvement and finish with elation.

Now I was finishing every run deflated. I was missing bits here and there, one day on and two days off, and all the time I could feel my fitness disintegrating. Every day I went out running I knew there were only dregs of fuel left in the tank.

For the first week in June my diary entries got progressively more depressing. Stopped after 20 minutes; pain getting worse; felt terrible. Then on June 10th I just left the diary blank, and it stayed that way for the rest of the year. I simply abandoned it. I didn't want to write down one more word about my running. There's a limit to the amount of times you can record disappointment.

This was the first time since I started writing the diaries with Joe Doonan back in 1988 that I'd stopped putting anything into them. That's how far off the map I'd gone. My whole life had lost direction.

It was now three months before the start of the Sydney Olympics. The media circus that goes with the Olympics was already in full swing and every conversation about the Irish prospects included my name. Catherina McKiernan, some said, sure she only has to show up to win a medal.

I'd been preselected to compete for Ireland the previous year. Normally that's an honour, and a great sense of security for the athlete. As far as the Olympic Council were concerned I was going to be the first person on the plane to Sydney. I was thinking the opposite. The only ticket I was interested in was one that could get me out of Sydney.

Another race had been planned for the end of June 2000. My back was still causing problems but because I could still run through the pain there wasn't really any great reason to withdraw. Not yet anyway. At least that's what people around me were saying.

All my races were set up by my agent, Ray Flynn. He worked closely with my brother Peadar, who from early in my career was also my manager. I'd been invited to a special event in Sweden, a once-off road race to celebrate the opening of a new suspension bridge. We agreed it was probably best to go. Sometimes a good race can help turn around even the worst situations.

Joe and I travelled up to Copenhagen, then on to Malmö for the start. The journey up there I can remember but what happened from there on has become a blur. I know it involved a certain amount of tears and the realisation that I would not be running in the Sydney Olympics.

After the journey home, Damien was there in Dublin airport to collect us. I couldn't even talk to him. So, he said, how did you get on?

I just sort of frowned and shook my head. That's all I could do. Damien had no idea where I finished, or even if I finished.

It was probably the only time in my life when I was completely lost for words. I was just so dazed. Driving back I still couldn't say a word. I knew I wasn't going to be running in the Olympics. To me that was a relief, but I still couldn't deal with the fact that I had to tell everyone. I just couldn't grasp any way of saying that out loud. Not yet anyway.

Right there and then I knew I wanted nothing whatsoever to do with running. I never wanted to race again, anywhere. And nobody was going to tell me otherwise.

Joe was trying to tell Damien not to worry, that I'd done okay. What he really meant was don't ask.

As we drove home, the silence in the car was broken by the ringing of Damien's mobile phone. At last, some distraction! It turned out to be some enthusiastic journalist wanting to know where I'd finished. Damien, already well versed in these cover-ups, said I wasn't too disappointed and mentioned something about blisters. Ah yes, blame it on the blisters.

The truth is I was totally burnt out. Fed up, had enough – whatever way you want to say it. I had cracked, and it had nothing to do with pressure. I think pressure means so many different things to different athletes. I'd never worried or even cared about pressure. There was big pressure on me going into the London marathon two years earlier and I didn't lose a minute's sleep over it. In a way you can only generate pressure on yourself, and eventually I did that in the months leading up to Sydney.

It wasn't like I felt under any pressure to go there and deliver anything in Sydney, that the whole country would be disappointed if I didn't. It just didn't work that way with me. I knew myself I wasn't going to run there and didn't care if I never raced anywhere again. But there was a different sort of pressure on me now, over how and when I was going to break this news. And I couldn't handle that for much longer.

A week later, at the end of June, the Olympic Council had organised a parade of the new adidas gear to be worn in Sydney. I'd agreed several weeks beforehand to go along. If I'd had any sense left I would have stayed at home but I clearly had very little sense left.

It was a beautiful summer's day at the Radisson St Helen's Hotel on the Stillorgan Road in Dublin. There was a real Olympic buzz in the air that day. About a dozen Irish athletes modelled the gear. I'd never faked so many smiles in the one day. I stood there all afternoon with a face like a mask. I couldn't get out of there quick enough. I ran straight for my car and drove home. I couldn't play this game any longer.

That evening I called around to Damien's family house in Castleknock and told him straight up. There was just no way I was going to the Olympics, that was it. I don't think he really knew what to make of it.

For the next few days Damien was still urging me on, trying to persuade me to change my mind. Don't be hasty, he'd say. Just take another day to think about it. I could understand what he was trying to do, but he didn't realise just how low things had fallen in my running career.

It was only then I fully realised that this was going to be a big disappointment to a big number of people. To my mother and father and all the family and all the relations around Cavan and around the country. To all the sponsors and friends and supporters who'd backed me down the years – the very people I thought about every time I pulled on the green vest of Ireland. To the people I was always running for, just to see the smiles on their faces, to give them something to celebrate. And beyond them, out on the roads and in the shops, to every single person I met who would ask me the same question. So are you looking forward to Sydney?

Ah, sure I don't know. I just don't know.

Of course you are! You've plenty of time to get ready. Don't be talking like that.

I felt like everybody around me was trying to convince me that I had to go. But all I wanted to hear was one person tell me I shouldn't go. Not to worry about it, that I didn't have to go. Forget about it. Not one person was able to say that to me.

It reached the stage where I could practically hear people talking behind my back. Jesus, sure she'll have to go. She'll have to be there. She'll never know unless she goes. All that kind of thing.

Joe came on the phone and told me to take another week to think about it. I knew I'd done all the thinking I could do.

A few days later, on a sunny Saturday morning, and having told Damien a couple more times, I completely let it go. He and Peadar had both come down to the house to try and figure something out. Peadar tried to put it to me one more time, to keep going a while longer, but before he could even finish I just stood up.

I'm not going to the bloody Olympics, I said.

And that was it. I instantly felt a huge sense of relief. I knew I'd made one of the most important decisions of my life, but in the end it was one of the easiest, for the simple reason that I had no choice. I was so far removed from all the reasons I started to run in the first place, and the reasons why I loved to run. Why I could go out on a Sunday morning and run for two hours and never realise the time. Why an open field and a warm breeze and the smell of freshly cut grass were to me a running paradise calling.

Those days were gone. I'd run to the end of the line. Instead of running being my life, I was now running for my life, and running scared. I'd run out of control. I didn't like that anymore and I had a hard time imagining that I'd ever make it back to where it all began.

Most athletes would need to be tied down and tranquillised before being told they weren't going to the Olympics: Such a disappointment, such a setback, after so much hard work. I viewed it in total contrast. To me there was no disappointment. I'd made the decision myself. No one needed to explain it to me. In the end it was my only choice. There were still two months to go before the Olympic flame even arrived in Sydney, and maybe I could have turned it around, but I'd been tormented long enough.

Peadar agreed to announce my decision officially on the Monday. By lunchtime some of the local radio stations were running the news and by teatime I'd say the whole country had heard.

I got a call from Yvonne Judge, a producer at RTÉ radio. I'd got to know Yvonne over the years and agreed to talk about it that evening on *Sportscall*, where listeners call in from around the country and talk about the main stories of the weekend.

The presenter, Des Cahill, came on and no doubt expected me to be weeping down the line, holding back the tears as if my whole world had ended. I don't think he could figure out why I sounded so relieved. In the end Des just tried to console me, offering the commiserations of the nation, that kind of thing. He was very nice about it, but the most ironic thing was that I was totally relieved the news was out there, and delighted with the decision I had made.

That's how ridiculous it had become. The whole country was probably feeling sorry for me, and yet I felt as if the weight of the world had been lifted off my shoulders. Such relief, such freedom. These were the most pleasant days of my life in a long time.

I didn't mean to sound ungrateful in any way when I said that not going to Sydney was something I'd get over, but I'd been to two Olympics and that was experience enough. So there was no way I wanted to go to Sydney unless I knew I was ready to put myself through another marathon and was going to run well. They were the two essential ingredients and both were missing.

Running a marathon when I wasn't fit enough would have been foolish beyond all reason. I could understand why a lot of people were upset for me. It was less than two years since I'd run the sixth-fastest women's time in history – two hours, 22 minutes, 23 seconds – to win the Amsterdam marathon in November of 1998. And my victories in Berlin and London in the 12 months before that were still fresh in the minds of a lot of people.

I should have taken a good break after those three marathons. I was asking for trouble by going straight back into intense training. But that's exactly what I did. Amsterdam was on November 1st 1998, and there was a perfect opportunity to take a good, long break and stay fresh for the Olympics in 2000. I missed that opportunity and paid a heavy price.

As a result every bit of hunger I had left to train hard was gone at a time when I needed it most. For a year or two I had been training on the edge, constantly pushing myself to the limit. I think the only people who really understand what it's like to train on the edge like that are the people who've pushed themselves over it.

It just felt like there was very little left to run for in my life. I'd never run for any material rewards, least of all money. At that stage running had given me everything I wanted in life and I'll always appreciate that. But if it was money that was motivating me I would have gone on to run another marathon before the end of 2000 and leeched the situation for all it was worth.

There's a lot of money floating around those big-city marathons, but I was never tempted by any of it. I tried to explain this to Joe Doonan quite a few times, and anyone else who wanted to know, that I don't really run these races for myself, and that I was always happy to run just for the joy it brought. Everything else – the money, the medals and the trips to the Olympic Games – that was all for the family, for the friends.

What depressed me most about pulling out of Sydney wasn't missing out on the medals or the chance to run for Ireland or even the money at the end of it all. It was just missing out on the daily runs, that I just wasn't able to go out the door and enjoy all that freedom I'd cherished since I was a child.

I could never have imagined how down I would feel once I realised that joy of running was gone. I was depressed that I wasn't able to run, and depressed with myself for allowing such pressure to build up on me. I would often ask myself how I could have allowed it go so far. If there is a price to pay for every success story this was it.

Released from this pressure of running in Sydney I realised the injuries were just pointers towards the real problem. Some athletes when they retire don't care if they ever run again. I could never feel that way. Somewhere along the line I'd started to get the balance wrong and my first step back was to try to restore that balance.

It's a hard thing to explain, but I knew that running had got me into this situation and only running could get me out. It was something I couldn't live without.

As the Sydney Olympics approached I knew with even greater certainty that the thought of missing out on a medal wasn't the source of my misery.

I didn't hear from Joe Doonan for a while. I knew what he was thinking, that when I was ready to get back training I'd just call him and resume duties. He knew that if the hunger was gone nothing he said could make me want to run.

Towards the end of July RTÉ offered me a position as one of their co-commentators in Sydney. They were planning their most extensive Olympic coverage ever and reckoned if I wasn't running there then the next best thing would be to have me commentating. They'd cover all the travel and expenses and pay me for it as well. I'd much rather have stayed at home but I just found it hard to say no. For some reason I felt under pressure, as if I had to do it.

I had to find something to occupy my mind while I tried to sort out my running. And it wasn't the only decision I made. Damien and I had originally planned our wedding for the spring of 2001 – the year after the Olympics. Now I was ready to move on, and I wanted to get married right away. November 2000 was still the earliest we could pull the whole thing together. So November it would be.

The wedding planning had to be put on hold for the three weeks I was in Sydney. I wasn't a natural-born commentator. Quite the opposite, in fact, and it was hard work. I didn't really enjoy my time in Sydney. I didn't feel like mixing, and besides working with RTÉ I didn't do a whole lot else out there. I don't know if I would have felt any better or worse watching at home. I was really in a no-win situation. But I must say, the RTÉ people were great and as helpful as could be. I had some good laughs, and we enjoyed a few good nights out.

I shared the microphone with Greg Allen of RTÉ radio on the Monday night of Sonia O'Sullivan's 5,000 metres final. I got very, very excited that night. When she came into the home straight I was actually standing up and shouting. Some people might think that must have been hard for me, watching Sonia win her Olympic silver medal. I was absolutely thrilled. I don't know what kind of person you'd have to be not to. And I believe she would have felt the same had the situations been reversed.

I saw Sonia briefly later that night. I just said well done. Nothing more. She just wanted to say something back, so she asked me how I was getting on with the radio work. Loving it, Sonia, just loving it, I told her. And we both laughed.

It didn't hurt at all. How could it? If my heart was really in the running at the time and if I was heartbroken at not making it to Sydney then I probably would have felt a small bit of envy, and it probably would have hurt.

But my heart wasn't in running. I was very happy for Sonia. I think her silver medal did spark something other than envy inside me. Sonia was born two days before me in 1969. In 2000 we were both 30 years old. I realised she'd risen above lots of disappointments to get back to the highest level.

Now it was my turn to discover if I could do the same. I had to at least try to regain some control of my running.

CHAPTER 2
GIRL OF THE NORTH COUNTRY

RUNNING WAS THE FARTHEST THING FROM MY MIND FOR several weeks after I returned home from the Sydney Olympics. As I expected, sitting in the commentary box and not being able to run wasn't any fun. Once I got home though I still needed to get out most days. I would head into the Phoenix Park and try to get around for at least 40 or 50 minutes. I just didn't have the enthusiasm or the interest to run much beyond that.

I had no idea if or when I would ever feel like training hard again. It was only a few weeks now before my wedding to Damien, and that was consuming most of my time.

What I did know was that there was no way I could train hard again unless I was enjoying my running. And that probably meant going back to where it all began – to cross-country. That's what brought me to the top of world athletics and perhaps it could take me there again.

I was born on November 30th 1969, the last of John and Kathleen McKiernan's seven children. Home was our 90-acre farm in Drumkeerin, Cornafean, about 10 miles outside of Cavan town.

It's been said a few times that the only people who've seen Cornafean are the ones who live there. Most of the time you wouldn't find Cornafean unless you knew exactly where you were going. It's a mile or so off the main road that heads from Cavan to Killeshandra. It's neither a village nor a hinterland. Cornafean is just a place, a locality, and the focal point is Tom McSeáin's pub, which nestles by the road and doubles as the local shop. When people come looking for directions to the pub they're usually told it's equidistant from Ballinagh, Arva and Killeshandra. That only confuses them further.

There's not much else to Cornafean now, except the pitch-and-putt course, which extends up the hills behind the pub, and a new community centre beside the GAA ground, Páirc Naoimh Fionnáin, which is below our house on the main Cavan-to-Arva road.

Our house lies at the top of a long, winding lane, which takes you to one of the highest points in Cornafean. Growing up in a quiet, rural place like that you take a lot of things for granted. Whenever people come to the house for the first time they usually spend the first few minutes taking in the panoramic views. On a clear day you can see as far as the hills of Meath and Fermanagh and into Leitrim, Longford, Westmeath and Monaghan. You can very clearly see Seán Quinn's wind turbines in Teemore, 13 miles away, over the Border in Fermanagh. I always took that view for granted.

I was two days old when I was first brought back to that house, and I didn't leave it until I was able to walk down the lane myself. That's the way we were all raised. None of my brothers and sisters – Thomas, Dympna, Peadar, Seán, Eileen and Rose – ever left that house either until they too were able to make their own way down the lane. Or so my mother told us anyway.

Our first venture was always to Mass on a Sunday. It wasn't an option, it was an obligation. The only exception was when one of the elder brothers or sisters would stay behind to mind the younger ones, until we were all able to go ourselves.

My father drove an old Volkswagen Beetle but my mother didn't drive at all. That made the transport system very simple. Unless my father had the time to drive us anywhere, which he rarely did, we would have to walk. Or else take one of the bikes that were lying around the yard.

Someone once traced the McKiernan family back to the nearby town of Gowna. We never had much reason to trace our family tree beyond that.

Outside of life working on the farm, Gaelic football was probably the other thing that mattered most to the McKiernan family, and especially to my brothers. My father's father won a county medal with Cornafean back in 1909, the club's first county title, and was always spoken about as a great footballer.

Although my father never really had much time to play football himself he was always a very fit man. He was consumed by the outdoor life and especially hunting. Most Sundays during the winter he would join in a beagle hunt, which he still does. He also had great natural strength and developed it from working on the farm, and I think I inherited some of that.

My mother always kept that house in great working order. The kitchen was the centre of our actions, a sort of command centre. We were entirely self-sufficient but that didn't make working around the house any easier. We grew all our own vegetables, which meant lots and lots of potatoes at every meal. We produced our own milk and our own eggs. Every now and then we'd kill an animal, and that meant there was always enough meat in the freezer to satisfy our needs.

Money was never a major issue with us. Times weren't always easy but were never too tough. My father worked hard for everything he got. When we kept pigs he would regularly bring the young litters into the market at Arva. He would head off determined to get say £10 apiece, and he'd sooner bring them home again than sell them at a reduced price.

Some people still think I put Cornafean on the map of Ireland. The truth is that Gaelic football put it there long before me. The club won 20 senior county titles, the first in 1909 and the last in 1956. When they won in 1936 and 1937 the star player was John Joe O'Reilly, who went on to captain the Cavan team that famously won the All-Ireland titles of 1947 and 1948, the first of which was played in the old Polo Grounds in New York. John Joe ended up winning 11 Ulster senior titles with Cavan. He died in 1952 and was named at centre back in the GAA Team of the Millennium in 2000.

While I was growing up, that football tradition in Cornafean thrived once again. My brothers Thomas and Peadar played for the club and county teams throughout the 1980s, when Cavan were managed by Eugene McGee, who had won an All-Ireland with Offaly.

That was always a great source of pride for my father, and he wasn't afraid to show it. He had a real competitive streak in him, and I know I inherited some of that too. One time Cornafean were playing Killygarry, and one of their players belted Peadar as they wrestled for the ball. My father didn't like to see that happening to Peadar and walked onto the pitch and made his views known very clearly to the match officials.

That was just the way John McKiernan stood up for his children. He was happy to let us run about and do our own thing but if there was any danger at hand he wasn't going to stand around and just watch. He'd be straight in to defend us. You could say he guarded us like a shepherd would his sheep.

Usually the youngest in the family is the most outgoing. I suppose I was the opposite. I was particularly shy, very quiet and very reserved. My brothers and sisters were happy to leave me to my own routine, because theirs was certainly different from mine. Come the weekend all they could talk about was where they were going on Friday and Saturday night, to the pub or the disco or wherever.

By the time my elder sisters were in the late teenage years everything about the house had changed. They would regularly go out with friends at the weekend. I never got into that scene – that's just the way I was. They would pay me to iron their clothes on a Saturday evening while they got ready to go out. And I was happy to do that.

Because it was such a small house we always had to put a list on the door of the bathroom, and if someone ever skipped his or her turn to take a bath or shower there would be war. And of course the hot water would always be gone before everyone was done. That used cause holy war. Then they'd all be gone out by around nine, off to the pub first, and I'd be in bed by 9.30. I was never even tempted to join them. I never felt like I was missing out on anything. My sisters were very close to me growing up.

All through my teenage years I didn't have the interest to go out chasing boys. By the time I got into my 20s I was so immersed in my running that I had no time at all. We had a television in the house but all we ever really watched was sport, the news and the odd soap.

When I was growing up, the great Kerry football team of the 1980s were at their peak, and that meant they were on television more than any other team. Pat Spillane was always my favourite player, and probably the best I have seen.

Many years later I was sitting in a London hotel for a press conference ahead of the 1998 London marathon. Most of the English journalists were having as hard a time finding questions to ask as I was answering them. Towards the end of it one of them asked me about my heroes when I was growing up.

Well, it would have to be Pat Spillane, I said. Yeah, Pat Spillane.

They just looked at me, clearly having no idea who I was talking about. They couldn't seem to swallow their pride and just ask. I think they just figured he was some famous Irish marathon runner they'd never heard of.

Could you spell that please?

I met Pat Spillane shortly after that in his pub in Kerry. He had heard about the press conference in London, and we had a good laugh about it.

And all my heroes growing up were sporting heroes – people like Daley Thompson and Steve Cram. Much later on in my career I met both of them too.

I find it funny sometimes how all the neighbours around Cornafean recall my younger days with such vividness, as if they knew this little girl running around the fields was destined to make her mark in sport. One story they love to tell is how they'd come visit my father and see me out in the field playing football or camogie, usually alone. And when they'd leave two hours later I'd still be at it.

Other times I'd have joined Peadar and Thomas in the football field down the end of the lane. I'd be kicking the ball up between them for what seemed like hours on end as they practised their fielding skills. And I'd still be sorry when it was time to go home.

Peadar was also known to go off on these long cycles into Arva, round to Killeshandra, and home again. It was well over 10 miles and I would always try to go with him. All we had at home then were man-sized bikes. When I was too small to ride them, I'd have to stick one leg under the crossbar and lean out to one side to ride the thing. But that never stopped me.

The silage-making season was my favourite time of the year. There was so much going on all around the farm, and everyone was working outside. There'd be three or four big tractors moving about and I wasn't afraid to help out there either. One time when the men were eating dinner I took off on a tractor and started bringing trailer loads of silage from the field to the pit in the farmyard. I don't know how old I was but they were happy to let me do it for the rest of the week.

For as long as I can remember I had a great love of the outdoor life, almost a fascination, and there's no doubt that contributed to my love of running. There were days in the spring and summer when I would be outside all day.

It was the same with everyone else in the family. At the start of each summer my father would take us up to Mullahoran, where there were banks of turf, which he would cut and save as fuel for the winter.

We'd head off early in the morning with a big flask of tea and sandwiches. What would usually happen was we'd get there and decide we'd have the tea and sandwiches first, before we got down to work. That was the excuse we'd use to put off the hard work for a while, but of course we'd be starving then for the rest of the day. I suppose working in the bog was my least-favourite outdoor activity. And I imagine anyone who has done it will understand.

When I started primary school in Coronea there were only four of us in the class – Joan McGahern, Deirdre Sheridan, Deirdre Martin and myself. We had no choice really but to get along very well, which thankfully we did. And there was nothing we all liked better than to just run around.

We had a game called tig, which more or less met our needs every day at lunchtime. It's a traditional childhood game that has survived purely because of its simplicity. One person would be nominated to be "on" at the start and if they touched someone ("tig") then that person was on. What I remember most about those games was the frustration of the other girls at not being able to catch me. Not even once.

Like most youngsters of that time and place I couldn't sit still for more than a minute. I had to be outside running about or occupying myself with some sort of physical activity.

By the time I started secondary school at Loreto, outside Cavan town, our lunchtime games had spread beyond tig. We'd play anything and everything from basketball to badminton. I was also taking gymnastics lessons. And I was getting particularly enthusiastic about camogie. Within a few months of starting at Loreto I was given special permission to eat my lunch during class because all the teachers knew I'd be too busy to eat anything during the break.

Although I was born in the country, it was much later in my life before I ever felt like I was born to run cross-country. Competitive running was one of the last sports I was drawn into. By the end of primary school the only sport I was becoming competitive in was camogie, which is always described to those who don't know it as hurling for girls.

With only four of us in my primary-school class there simply weren't enough young girls around Cornafean to start up a camogie team. So we used to play for the neighbouring club Killeshandra. It was a few years after that when we managed to get a club team going in Cornafean. My three sisters, Dympna, Eileen and Rose, also played on the team, and I usually played at midfield with Eileen. I was also the designated free-taker. We took it very seriously and were soon winning games as a matter of habit. I believe that's where I developed my competitive edge.

It reached the stage where all I did after school was play camogie. The club team had gone from novice to senior in just a few years, and everyone from around Cornafean would come to see us play. One of the games I'll never forget was a senior championship match against Kill, who were one of the best teams in the county. We'd matched them play for play but Kill were up by two points as the game spilled into extra time. Just as I was thinking they were going to win this game no matter what, we were awarded a free. The referee pointed at the watch to indicate it would be the last puck of the game, so it had to be a goal or nothing. I just lined up the ball and sent it thundering into the back of the net. I still get a real rush of adrenaline when I think about that game.

Camogie was my main sport right through secondary school in Loreto Cavan. The school team was also becoming quite successful, and we'd train two or three days in the week. As well as that I started training with the county team during the summer. With the bright evenings I'd cycle the eight miles into Cavan for training and then cycle home again afterwards.

During the school year I'd have to take the school bus into Cavan every morning, and home again in the evening. I dreaded that journey. I would have much preferred to cycle it, or even run it. Some days I'd deliberately miss the bus and would have to take the bike.

It wasn't until my Intermediate Certificate year that I first became involved in any sort of competitive running. No one else in my family was ever involved in running. Instead it all started with the few girls in my class who would go cross-country training at lunchtime. Around that time the schools competition was coming up, and when I was asked to join them one day I didn't have to think twice about it.

I'd already run in a few small races over the years. As with most children growing up in Ireland, the Community Games provided my first lesson in competition. But unlike many of those who went on to be international athletes, I didn't win gold at the Community Games.

My first and only experience was with the county finals, which were held at Breffni Park GAA grounds in Cavan. I was so shy that I wouldn't even go to the starting line unless my sister Eileen held my hand. They weren't letting anyone else into the field except the runners, and of course I started crying. Poor Eileen was totally embarrassed by the whole thing.

Somehow they got me to the start line, and when the whistle blew I took off like a hare. I had no idea how to run a race, so of course one of the other girls caught me, and I came in second. But at least I'd won out against the shyness. If it weren't for the running, I don't think I would ever have got over it, the shyness that is.

My first real success was in the Ulster Novice cross-country in Kill in 1987. It was a cold, wet day, and as usual Eileen and Dympna and Rose had to come along to lend support. I was so cold standing around before the start that I went off and ran for 25 minutes. When I got back they were mad at me for running so much before the race, thinking there was no way I'd win it now. They weren't even going to get out of the car to watch.

One of the best girls around at the time was Niamh O'Reilly, the local favourite and a friend of mine, and she was expected to win. I don't know whether I was angry because my sisters were angry, but I was determined to win it, and I did. That was probably the day I discovered my running talent was as good as anything else around. It was definitely the day I discovered the thrill of winning.

That was during my fourth year at secondary school, and later on in the season I qualified to run for Loreto in the All-Ireland Schools cross-country, to be staged at the Mallusk course, just outside of Belfast. I was well beaten that day by another young girl that I'd never heard of before. Afterwards we were told she was from Cobh, Co Cork, and her name was Sonia O'Sullivan.

I never met Sonia that day, and didn't realise for quite a while afterwards that we'd first raced together so early in our careers. Although we were the same age, she was finishing at school that summer, and I had another year to go, because I hadn't started school until I was almost six. My mother kept me home for an extra year because I was small for my age and she decided I wasn't ready for the daily walk – three miles in all – to and from Coronea school.

But it wasn't like I left Mallusk thinking I would come back and win the following year. I never thought like that. I just loved to run, and at that stage of my career I didn't really care where I finished. It was only when I did begin to win that pressure came on me to keep winning. It just so happened that I started to win races solely because I was a good runner, and not because I'd ever planned to win.

By the time I started my Leaving Cert year my love of running was complete and had almost taken me over. We were warned that year to study every day after school but I could never study for too long without thinking about running.

I'll always remember when I was studying for my Leaving they started cutting the silage, and the fields were a beautiful, open stage for running. At least three or four times a day I'd take a break from the studying and go out and run for 15 or 20 minutes. I loved that. The fresh air, the freshly cut grass – it was heaven. When I'd come back in I could concentrate a bit better on the books.

There were still days around that time when I'd just jump on the bike and head off for maybe two hours, miles away. When I came back I'd go running around the fields for 30 minutes, and then in the evening I'd head off for camogie training. I always seemed to have the energy for it. I can't remember it any other way. I realised it was a little unusual, and none of the other girls around would be nearly as active.

I'd somehow become addicted to running, and I couldn't explain why. All I knew was that I'd be like a demon at the end of the day if I didn't get a run in. I'd run anywhere. Sometimes I'd go down to the GAA pitch at the end of the lane and just run around and around that for 35 or 40 minutes. I'd never get bored and I'd only go home because I had to. And I had absolutely no idea at the time but I was building the foundation of a great running career.

My father was always happy to let me do my own thing. But my mother always said I was too hard on myself and should rest more instead of being out running around for so long. Some days I'd come home from school and it would be lashing rain, but I'd be straight out of the uniform and into the running gear. You can't go out in that, my mother would say. You'll catch your death. Ah, I'll be grand. And off I'd go.

But in the early days I would never run on the roads around home, purely out of shyness. For a start there was no one else doing it. So I'd run around the fields at the back of the house and down on the football pitch where no one could see me.

During the winter it would be as black as coal outside the house from five o'clock onwards. There was no way you could run around the roads or fields after that, at least not without some company, but most evenings at around eight I'd get this notion that I wanted to go running. That just wasn't the done thing back then, to go running around the country roads in the dark. You wouldn't even go out for a walk at night. Most people had been working hard on the farm all day and all they wanted to do was have a nice rest in front of the fire.

Eileen didn't have her own car then, but I eventually got her to go out with me on the bike. She bought this big torch especially for that purpose and would tie it onto the front of the bike. So I'd go running up the road for maybe a mile and a half, and then back. That was always great fun.

The only problem was I would have to stop every time a car passed by. I didn't want to be seen running. Because it was so hilly around those roads, if Eileen stopped she found it hard to get going again. So one night she got totally fed up with this. She just shouted at me to keep going, that if I stopped one more time she would never come out with me again. That did the trick alright and as time went on nothing would stop me.

Midway through my last year in school there was an incident that I now know was the turning point in my running career and, as it turned out, the single most important turning point in my life. It was when running was turned from a pastime to a present time, when I discovered some ambition beyond the basic desire to go fill my lungs with air and cover the open ground. I suppose it was the end of my innocence.

CHAPTER 3
TWIST OF FATE

DURING MY LAST YEAR IN LORETO CAVAN I WAS MADE THE sports captain of my class, partly because of my success in camogie, and partly because most people who knew me at all knew how much I loved sport. The school had a very strong camogie team that year. I was the engine of the team at midfield, and probably one of the better players on the team.

As expected we progressed to the Ulster semi-finals, which were scheduled for the second-last weekend in February of 1988. Straight away I realised that was the same weekend as the Ulster Schools cross-country. I double checked the dates. The camogie match was on the Friday afternoon, and the cross-country was on the Saturday morning. There was no way I was going to play a camogie match the day before the race. It had to be one or the other.

I talked about it at home for a few nights with my father and mother, and it was quite obvious I wanted to run the cross-country. It was still a very tough decision for me to make, because I loved to play camogie whenever I could.

Something inside of me needed to find out if I could win the cross-country. What I didn't realise was how big a problem that was going to be for the school. In retrospect it's easy to understand the school's emphasis on team sports ahead of my own personal interests. But at the time I was solely focused on my own ambition. I decided not to play the match and opted to race instead. The school couldn't force me to play and I sensed I was very much letting it down.

What happened next was almost inevitable. The team went out on the Friday afternoon and lost. I went to the Ulster Schools cross-country in Mallusk on the Saturday morning and won.

It meant a lot to win that race. I'd prepared well for it and won well. I had proved myself the best schoolgirl runner in Ulster and in the process had qualified to run in the All-Ireland Schools cross-country in three weeks' time.

I didn't know what to expect going into school on the Monday morning. Straight away a few girls on the camogie team wouldn't talk to me. They just completely ignored me. So I was in a bad way by the time we got to class. After a few minutes I could hear one or two girls calling me traitor under their breath. And pretty soon I was crying.

Throughout the week the situation went from bad to worse, with misunderstanding piling up on misunderstanding, which eventually led to me being banned from training around the school grounds and being stood down as sports captain. There was even the possibility that I might not be allowed to run in the All-Ireland Schools cross-country.

My parents intervened with the school and shortly after that the whole incident got a national coverage in the *Irish Independent*. Its athletics correspondent, Tom O'Riordan, a journalist with a great reputation, and a former international runner, wrote about the proposed ban in his Friday column.

The school was soon deluged with calls from journalists wanting to know whether I was going to be allowed participate in the All-Irelands. What started as a minor disagreement had escalated into a major crisis for both the school and me. Thankfully, we managed to get the matter resolved to everyone's satisfaction and the school gave me its full blessing to compete in the All-Irelands.

All during this time I kept training every day. Nothing about the incident had hindered my desire to run. If anything it only heightened it. Once I got home from school I would run the distance of the All-Ireland event around the fields at the back of the house, about two miles. I was determined to win that All-Ireland title no matter what.

I often wondered afterwards what would have happened if the matter hadn't been resolved. There's every chance that I might never have run competitively again. You can only put moments like that down to destiny, or else luck.

I'll never forget the story Tom O'Riordan wrote. He would write hundreds more stories about me over the years but that one will always stand out.

Tom had obviously earned the respect of my parents as well. I was so shy over the years that whenever the phone rang in the house I had my mother well warned to say I wasn't around, especially if it was anyone from the media looking for me. But whenever Tom rang I would hear my mother say a few nice words and then say of course, Tom, she's right here beside me.

Still the whole hullabaloo of the camogie versus the running didn't end there, as I still had to run in the All-Ireland Schools cross-country. That was taking place in the grounds of St Augustine's College in Dungarvan, at least a four-hour journey from Cornafean and about as far as I'd ever been from home. Once the school agreed I could run I knew I had to win.

So the whole family got behind me on this adventure to Dungarvan. They all made it sound like a big deal just to get there, and that didn't do my nerves any good. The race was on a Saturday, and my father collected me straight after school on the Friday. He'd been at the mart in Cavan that afternoon. On my way out the door I met the head nun and she wished me luck.

My father took me out to the bus station in Cavan and sent me on my way to Dublin. My brother Peadar and sister Rose were both living in Dublin at the time and had arranged to meet me off the bus. My mother had already made my dinner for me and wrapped it up on a plate, and the smell of that was wafting all over the bus.

Rose was living in a flat out in Drumcondra, and I stayed the night there.

Peadar called around first thing in the morning and we headed off to Dungarvan. He had bought a new camera around that time, and on our journey to Waterford he would stop every so often to take pictures of the scenery. I was so anxious now I was sure I'd miss the race.

As soon as I saw the course, almost all the nerves disappeared. It was practically all flat and as smooth as a carpet. I was so used to running on hills that I knew this would be easy. And it was so dry I decided to leave my running spikes in my bag and run barefoot. I went to the start line wearing an old white T-shirt and wine-coloured shorts.

The best way to describe that race is to say I ran away with it. I led from the gun, and no one else got a look in. It was the first of my solo runs. I remember being interviewed shortly after the finish by the late Brendan O'Reilly from RTÉ. He asked me why I wasn't wearing any shoes.

Ah, the shoes felt too clobby, I said – in this thick Cavan accent.

I don't think he knew what to make of me. They showed that interview the following Saturday on the old *Sports Stadium* programme. I couldn't bear to watch it, and I would never get used to watching myself on television.

Whenever anything came on the television about me at home I would beg them to turn down the volume. My brothers and sisters have a whole box of videos of nearly all my main races but I hardly ever watched any of them. Now and again I do get to see some of them, and I do admire myself for how strong I was. I know I will appreciate those races more and more as the years go by.

Peadar got very excited by what he saw in Dungarvan that day. He obviously realised I had a talent for running and I think he decided he was going to help me develop it as best he could. That was the start of a special relationship with him, and he did help me in a great number of ways over the years. He took care of so many things around my running that it soon reached the point where he had effectively become my manager before either he or I realised it.

We still had to make it back to Cornafean. Peadar was reliving the race so many times that he wasn't concentrating on the driving at all, and we must have taken a wrong turn going through every town. We stopped off in Cashel at a friend of Peadar's for a feed of sausages and fried bread and eventually got home about 10 o'clock.

There's a big trophy for winning the Irish Schools title and I brought it into school on the Monday. It was left outside the head nun's office for the rest of the week, and it was also announced over the intercom that I had won.

Nothing about my running was ever the same again after I won that All-Ireland title in Dungarvan. In a way it took on a life of its own. At the time I had wanted to win that race more than anything. I had sacrificed my love of camogie, and running had obviously become the main focus of my life. And yet it wasn't the success that I craved. I simply loved to run.

But from now on it wasn't going to be that simple, and the very fact that I was successful meant that it wasn't just about me and my love of running any more. People deal with that situation in different ways. Some people embrace the success and walk towards it. Others shy away from it and eventually lose their interest in sport as a result. At the time, I felt like I was caught somewhere between the two.

Just a couple of weeks after I won the Irish Schools title I started receiving letters from various colleges in America. Some were sent to the school, others to the house, although I'd no idea how they tracked me down. Apparently there were a few scouts around the country who would send the names of potential recruits to various coaches in American colleges, who would then consider offering a scholarship. Young Irish athletes had been going to American colleges for years, starting with Jimmy Reardon and John Joe Barry in the late 1940s and continuing with Ronnie Delany and Frank Murphy, then Eamonn Coghlan and John Treacy, and more recently the likes of Marcus O'Sullivan and Frank O'Mara, and of course my collaborator on this book, Ian O'Riordan.

The American scholarship scene probably peaked in the late 1980s. The popular perception around then was that you had to go to America if you wanted to make it to the top of the sport. In terms of the coaching and the facilities and most of all the competition, America was light years ahead of Ireland.

It reached the stage that any athlete who was in any way ambitious about achieving anything in distance running had to go there. Those who decided to stay at home were more or less told they were taking the wrong option. And there were precious few athletes who had made any sort of major breakthrough after staying at home.

What people obviously didn't realise was that I had absolutely no intention of ever going to America. Still, one college in Dallas, Texas, was particularly eager to get me out there. Another one sent over a representative to meet me in person. I had no idea this recruiting business was so serious. I found it hard to say no straight away, and I certainly wasn't trying to lead them on in any way, but deep down I just knew there was no way I'd be able to handle being so far away from home.

My parents didn't try to influence me either way. I think they knew there was no way I was going to go. I don't think I resisted just because of my nature. I think I already believed that I would still be as successful as I wanted to be by training in Ireland. There's never been a moment in my life when I regretted not going to America, but I do think I could have been successful out there too. I think I would have adapted.

I did as well as I'd hoped to do in my Leaving Cert exams, but like most 18-year-olds I didn't have a definite career plan in mind. Nor did I feel like leaving home for college. In the end I decided on a one-year secretarial course at the College of Further Studies in Cavan town, which was part of a business-studies course. That way I could still live at home and do all the training I wanted.

And once the Leaving Cert was finished I had all the time I wanted to run. And I did a lot of running that summer. I also qualified to run with an Irish junior international team in Wales, my first trip overseas.

Naturally someone from the family had to come with me, and my father agreed. What I remember most about that trip was the journey back, where for some reason I was as seasick as you can possibly get. My poor father couldn't do anything and I weighed about five stone by the time we got home to Cornafean. My mother spent the next week trying to feed me back to full health.

By the end of the summer I already felt my running had progressed to a higher level. I started the secretarial course in September but that still left plenty of time for training, and the new cross-country season couldn't come around quick enough. The difference was that I'd be running with the seniors for the first time, and I wasn't so sure how big a jump that would be.

The first real test would be the National cross-country in February 1989, which was set for Killenaule in Co Tipperary. It was the longest race I'd run in my 19 years and, as I expected, the hardest one too. Still, I wasn't that far away from winning it.

The defending champion was Catherine Rooney, originally from Sligo but running with Blackrock in Dublin, and she was then aged 31. This time she took the silver medal but was only one second ahead of me. Christine Kennedy from Galway, who was actually 34 at the time, won the race. They were both respected and experienced runners, so I got plenty of encouragement from taking the bronze medal behind them.

I'd also been noticed for the first time. Very few people in Killenaule that day knew who I was. I looked about 13, and lots of people left that day talking about this promising young girl from Cavan. The race also earned me a place on the Irish senior team for the World Cross Country, which was being held up in Stavanger, Norway, a few weeks later.

By then I'd run quite a few times for Ireland, so getting a place on the team wasn't a huge deal. One of the trips away I'll always remember was an under-23 international cross-country in Holland. Also travelling with that team were Dave Carrie and John Downes, as well as Teresa Duffy from Belfast and Teresa McKenna from Monaghan. We had a hilarious time.

We left on the Friday evening, flew out to Amsterdam, and we three girls had pains in our faces from all the laughing. Dave Carrie and John Downes are two of the liveliest characters you could meet, and the whole thing was great fun. Everyone was so friendly and having a good time and I remember thinking if every trip was going to be like this it would be a great life. I've got to know Dave Carrie particularly well in recent years and he's as funny as ever, with a lovely Louth accent to boot.

I actually finished quite high up in that race in Holland. Of course there was no pressure at all then, but I came away thinking I could have won it if I'd had a little more experience. The local papers, the *Anglo Celt* and the *Cavan Leader*, made a big deal about me running so well for Ireland for the first time. Word of my progress seemed to be spreading fast.

The Irish team for the World Cross Country also came together for a training session in the Phoenix Park before we left for Stavanger. We did something like 10 times 300 metres around the Polo Grounds, and it felt very easy to me. At least I knew I was in as good a shape as any of the other Irish girls.

As it turned out, the World Cross Country was a tougher experience than I'd even imagined. I'd never run a race of such importance and from the starting gun there were always people around me, and I just wasn't used to that. I've always hated being surrounded by other runners and I didn't realise then that the best way to get around them was to get in front of them.

It was also very, very muddy. It was raining and snowing the day before and that didn't exactly inspire me. I never got into the sort of rhythm I wanted to and ended up 76th. Christine Kennedy had finished 33rd and Catherine Rooney 64th.

Initially I was a little disappointed but it had been a priceless experience and I knew it would stand to me. I wasn't daunted either by what I saw – I knew I was standing at the doorway of further improvement. But I still can't say I have fond memories of my first World Cross Country. It was a strange place with some strange people, and I found the whole thing a little too serious. We stayed in the heart of the city and I was afraid to go out for a run in case I got lost, and I didn't enjoy being trapped like that.

A few weeks after that race, in April of 1989, I started two weeks' work experience at Tom Fitzpatrick's (solicitors) office in Cavan. That went well and they agreed to take me on for the summer. I enjoyed the work. There wasn't much pressure but it definitely took my mind off running when I needed to.

In September, Cavan County Council held exams for a couple of new openings. Those openings didn't come along very often and there were a large number of applications. I sat the exams and a few weeks later I was offered one of the jobs. I still think I jumped the queue a little bit, simply because I'd established a bit of a name for myself locally through the running. The county manager, Brian Johnston, was particularly good to me and would soon become one of my chief supporters.

That was another turning point in my career that I can only put down to destiny, or else luck. I was definitely lucky that Brian was a Cavan native and also had a strong interest in sport. If he'd said to me I needed to concentrate fully on the job and would have to forget about my running, then I think I might well have left the running behind me. Jobs like that weren't at all easy to get in 1989. It would have been such a big thing to turn down a job like that, I just don't think I would have been able to say no, or even tried to justify to myself and my family why running was more important.

If the county manager had been from another part of the country, I don't think he would have cared one bit about my running career. But from the very start Brian did. He gave me time off to train or race whenever I needed it. If anything, he encouraged me to run more. He just liked to see another person from Cavan doing well.

When I think about that situation now I know how fortunate I was. I wonder too how many athletes have lost out on sporting careers of one sort or another because of similar situations that just didn't work out in their favour.

So I was lucky the way things worked out there, and lucky to be so happy with my set-up just a year or so after leaving school. I was happy with my job and happy to be still living at home and happy with my training environment.

My father and mother continued to be very supportive of my running, but they also kept their distance. My father made sure I never got any more or less attention, and that suited me fine, because I hated being the centre of attention in any situation. My mother would always have dinner ready in the evening with freshly baked bread, but that was with the six others in mind as much as myself. I was never singled out for special treatment, and that was the way I wanted it.

By that time too I was also getting all the coaching and guidance I needed from Joe Doonan. He was now my coach, and I was now his athlete. Almost everything about my running was done as a team, and it stayed that way for the best part of the next decade.

Again, when I think about it now I don't know if it was destiny or luck that brought Joe and myself together. I do know that our meeting wasn't just another turning point but one of the most significant ones of my career.

CHAPTER 4
NO ORDINARY JOE

THE FIRST THING JOE DOONAN SAID TO ME ABOUT MY RUNNING was to hold back, that I was doing too much. From the time I was 15 or 16 I would get the urge to go out running two and sometimes three times a day. He told me once a day was more than enough.

Like so much else about my running career, what happened with Joe Doonan and myself didn't happen by my own design. It was never my plan or ambition to have a coach who would become so influential that it seemed like we were totally reliant on each other. And no one else planned it that way either. It happened almost by accident.

One night after I'd won the Ulster Novice cross-country in 1987 some of us were sitting in the kitchen and talking with a neighbour of ours, Fr Oliver O'Reilly. He was just back from a missionary trip to Africa, and he got very excited when he heard about my newfound success with the running.

So who's coaching you?

Ah no one, I said, sure I don't need a coach.

Of course you do, and I know the very man.

Fr Oliver had been in secondary school with Joe, and they'd kept in touch over the years. He started talking about Joe's interest in athletics and knowledge of coaching. Joe sounded like a very important person and I couldn't imagine why he'd want to coach me, but before I could say anything Fr Oliver had ducked out into the hallway to call Joe.

That's settled then, he said. Just call over to Joe on one of the evenings and he'll chat away about the running with you.

Joe lived in Carrigallen, about eight miles from Cornafean and just inside the Leitrim border. My mother and father had never met him and didn't seem to know anything about him. He was headmaster in the local national school and, from what Fr Oliver was saying, a big name in Irish athletics.

My sister Eileen agreed to drive me there the following Friday evening. Of course I was dreading it, just like I did anytime I had to meet a complete stranger. We didn't really know where we were going either but eventually we found his house.

Joe introduced his wife, Sheila, who had just cooked up a big dinner. Tea was poured and Joe started asking a few simple questions about what I was doing and what I wanted to do. I can't even remember what my first impression was because I was way too shy.

Without Eileen there I probably wouldn't have said anything. I did tell him how I might just take a notion and go out running in the back fields, maybe twice or three times a day. I was still so nervous about it I was only half listening to him. I do remember him saying I was doing too much running, and that I shouldn't be going out more than once a day, but to keep up the other sports as well.

He also wrote down a rough schedule, what I should be doing every week, with the main thing being only one run a day. I was to try it for a week and to call him next Sunday evening.

Grand, I said. What time?

Sunday night, he said.

Anyone who lived in Ireland in the 1980s will know all about *Glenroe*, possibly the most popular soap ever produced by RTÉ television. Over the next few months I slowly developed a fear and loathing of the theme music from Glenroe. It meant it was time to pick up the phone and call Joe. I dreaded those calls. I didn't enjoy talking to anyone on the telephone. Talking to a stranger such as Joe Doonan was a total nightmare. At that stage no one would ever have believed I would get a job as telephonist with Cavan County Council.

Anyway, after much procrastination, the call eventually happened.

So how did you get on this week?

Ah, fine, I'd say. And then he'd just run through what I should do the following week, and I'd write it down on a piece of paper. End of conversation.

Getting to know Joe in any sort of way was a slow and demanding process, and he probably thought the same about me. We met up a few times over the summer of 1988 when I finished with school, but he was still quite heavily involved elsewhere in Irish athletics at the time. He'd been working with the Irish Olympic team and was heading to the Seoul Olympics later that year.

When I started doing the secretarial course in Cavan he came down one day and we laid out a loop around the golf course, which is maybe five minutes out the road from Cavan town. No more than about 100 metres of that golf course is flat, and the rest is all hills. So essentially it was a loop of hills, which took about three minutes to run. I'd start on the flat, run downhill, across another flat part, and then up another steep hill. I always did that run on my own.

Whenever Joe did come down to watch me do a session, he would do nearly all the talking. And that suited me fine. He wasn't the kind of person that went around saying great things about you – like you were going to win this or that. In fact he never mentioned anything about what he thought I could do.

We'll just stick to this training, he'd say, and we'll see what happens. And that was a good attitude to have. He wasn't trying to build me up in any way, such as talking about the Olympics or anything like that.

Gradually we began to meet for training more often. By September of 1989 I was more or less doing exactly what he said I should be doing, except of course I would still do a little bit more. If Joe told me to run for 45 minutes at lunchtime I would run for 50. If he told me to run for an hour, I'd run for an hour and five minutes. For some reason I had to add on a few minutes more – it was just in my nature.

At the beginning I never found that training hard. I enjoyed it and would push myself most days without ever needing to be told. Some days were harder than others but I'd be out in all weathers and at all times of day and I never once questioned what I was doing. I developed a love for hard training from the very beginning.

Around that time Joe also started coming down to the football pitch in Cornafean. That's where he introduced me to some special training methods, and in particular the bounding exercises. Joe had a whole range of bounding exercise based around running and jumping on the spot, and that was something he would carefully develop with me over the years. We'd also go into the small changing area beside the pitch, which is literally a box room, and do some medicine-ball work. Some nights he'd come back up to the house for a cup a tea, and so he slowly got to know my parents who clearly both respected and trusted him.

Between the sessions on the golf course and the bounding sessions in Cornafean I was seeing Joe at least two or three times a week. He was coaching a few other athletes at the time, one of whom was Patricia Griffin, the wife of the former Irish athletics president Pádraig Griffin. He also had a few more young athletes from his school and from around where he lived.

During that first year or so he brought me over to the golf course in Ballinamore, where Patricia lived, to do a session with her. It was the first time I trained with anyone else, and the only time during those early years. She was much older than me and had just won the Women's Mini Marathon in Dublin, which to me seemed like a very big deal. Joe had this hill session planned and told me to just hang in with Patricia. The truth is I found it very, very easy. I was just tipping along, and this was meant to be a hard session.

After my third place in the National cross-county of 1989 the coach-athlete arrangement was almost complete. Joe was putting more and more thought into my training sessions, and he started to work almost exclusively with me. It was clear he knew exactly what he was doing and exactly what he wanted.

Towards the end of 1989 the training had become very structured and was clearly working. At the end of November I won the National Intercounties cross-country on Dundalk racecourse, and won it well. After that I was expected to win the National Interclubs title, which was set for the University of Limerick the following February.

It wasn't quite as comfortable as we though it would be, but I won by four seconds from Róisín Smyth of Derry, who was then the national 3,000 metres champion. It was my first national senior title and I was 20 years old.

I could tell Joe was quite pleased to see me win, but we still didn't say much afterwards. That was to become the norm. We did go off for something to eat after the race. At that stage all I was really eating – like all the McKiernan family – were potatoes, vegetables and meat, and lots and lots of them. I was brought up on them and loved them, and I saw no reason to be eating anything else.

We headed off to this restaurant and Joe ordered spaghetti. Now I'd never even seen spaghetti before, let alone eaten it.

This is what you'll have to eat from now on, said Joe. It's got lots more carbo-hydrate than potatoes.

What? You can't be eating that for your dinner, that's not real food.

Anyway, we agreed I should try it. I just didn't know how good it was for runners. We'd certainly never cooked spaghetti in our house, but the next week I went off and bought a few packets. I was boiling the water and cooking it on my own, and then sitting down to eat it.

Now that was a big issue at home. No one in the house had ever eaten the stuff. They were more than happy with their potatoes. Except some of the nieces and nephews loved it, like my eldest nephew, Shane Finnegan, who'd come down on a Sunday evening when I was cooking it – he'd always have to get some.

It was also Joe's idea around that time I start eating liver as well. It was great for the iron levels in the blood, he said. My mother would do her best to cook it up nicely but I was happy to throw it into me and not even think about it.

Joe had seven children, all of whom were younger than me. One of his sons, Brian, used to do a bit of race walking, but none of his children ever got into the running in a big way. He would often talk about his five daughters.

His motto was nothing would be gained without hard work. That was the way he taught me.

He took me to Trinity College for various physiological tests and started using heart-rate monitors before that sort of equipment became standard. When it came to athletics he was largely self-taught. He'd read and absorb almost anything he could get his hands on and would carefully separate the good from the bad.

While I trusted the training sessions he gave me and was happy to do them, no one else was having any other kind of input whatsoever.

Early in the summer of 1991 John Treacy, Ireland's silver medal winner in the

1984 Olympics in Los Angeles, was back in Ireland and I met up with him a few times. He looked through a couple of my training diaries and was keen for me to go to America with him and run some track races over there. I'd spend something like six weeks out there and get a good block of training as well. But Joe was having none of that. Deep down I wasn't too keen myself.

Joe's main method of coaching was to work back from the race day and write out the training schedules in reverse. I stuck rigidly to those training schedules. I'm sure there were mistakes made along the way but I'd have to take some of the blame for that too. There were some days when I was really too tired to train, but I would usually get on with it anyway. I don't know if that was any benefit at all. I think if I had been a little older and wiser I definitely would have questioned it, because there are definitely days when your body is just too tired to train and will get absolutely no benefit from it no matter how hard you push. It would be more like de-training, if such a term exists. At the time I didn't realise that.

Throughout those early years we never talked about much at all, just a few words about the training. On the days he'd meet me in Cornafean I'd have warmed up by the time he got there, so I'd be ready and waiting to start into the bounding.

He would arrive in at the pitch. Pulse! That was all he'd say to me. And I'd say 38. Other days I'd ring him when he wanted to know how a session went. Pulse! Again that was the first word he'd say to me. So once the pulse rate was down where he wanted it he was happy, because it meant I wasn't sick or over-training or anything like that.

Pulse! And he'd follow that by saying 28 – which meant the bounding exercises were based on 28 repetitions that evening.

Joe used to say the bounding exercises made me different from every other runner. And made me a better runner. Bounding is a plyometric exercise. It is hard work and a real test of endurance.

It definitely presented the most physical hardship of all the training. You'd end up working practically every muscle in your body. So the best part was always getting through it. It was definitely a challenge. But when I was really fit I'd almost be able to enjoy it.

In relatively simple terms, plyometric exercise is the method of training which attempts to enhance the explosive reaction of the athelete through muscular contractions. Bounding is essentially a form of plyometric exercise, which athletes had been using for years. I know Sebastian Coe did a lot of them in his day.

Our bounding sessions changed from week to week depending on what stage I was at in the training, or if a race was coming up. So the bounding could be off 26, 28, or 30 or whatever. In fact 32 repetitions was the highest.

There were six different exercises I had to do, and everything was four times by 28. I used to start with single-leg hops, just hopping on one leg, 28 times. Then I'd jog around for 10 seconds and it was straight into exercise number two – pogo jumps, and another 28 of those. Then there was the long stride. Then I'd kick my legs up behind me, like footballers do. And then a sort of high kick in front of me. And I'd finish off with jumps on the spot.

We had 10 seconds between each exercise, and 30 seconds between each set. That was a typical bounding session for the night.

I think the bounding did create a bit of an aura around my training, perhaps even instilled an extra bit of fear into my opponents.

But what made me the runner I was had a lot more to do with the amount of training I did on hills. In fact I was nearly always running up and down hills, and very rarely on the flat. Even a 40- or 50-minute run in the morning would always be over the hills.

One of my first trips down to Dublin was a photo shoot in the Phoenix Park, and I headed off for a run afterwards. It just didn't feel the same when I was done because it was nearly all on the flat. Every time I went out at home, there was a challenging hill somewhere. I think that's really what made me different. There was no cross-country course too tough for me after all the running I used to do on the hills.

Of course it was often wet and muddy around Cavan as well, so when we got to a nice, dry cross-country course I used to love it. For some reason I became known as one of these runners that loved the mud, just like John Treacy when he was winning the World Cross Country in 1978 and 1979. The truth is I hated running in the mud and I don't think that John liked it very much either despite his successes in the muck and rain of Glasgow and Limerick race-courses. When I moved to Dublin in the summer of 1997 I started to see less and less of Joe, and the ironic thing was we got on better as a result. I was becoming a little more independent, and with that I found it easier to talk with Joe.

We definitely had a different sense of humour. Joe was very intelligent and very well read, and would have an interest in subjects and topics that I wouldn't have any interest in. That was obviously one reason why we never had much to talk about. But Joe could be very funny at times, and it wasn't like we never enjoyed ourselves.

One such occasion that always stands out was in Chicago in 1999 when I was running my fourth marathon. A big group of us from Cavan were in the hotel bar, along with Joe and his wife, Sheila. People like Tom Clerkin, who was a good friend of Joe and travelled to many of my races. Damien's brother Kenneth and his friends Owen McConnon from Lavey and Declan Woods from Killeshandra had also travelled over. I also remember the Cavan footballer Jason O'Reilly was there with his girlfriend. As the drink flowed, Owen took the stage to sing, and Joe soon joined him on the guitar. We took over the whole bar and had a great night.

But when it got to the training it was mostly deadly serious. When Noel Berkeley started training with us he used to refer to Joe as Papa Joe. Joe was the boss, but Noel was well able to argue with him and ask him why we were doing certain sessions. I remember being horrified at seeing Noel question him.

A lot of people described our relationship as like that of a teacher and a pupil, though he didn't like that either. But to me that was the obvious way of describing it.

I sensed as well that when I moved to Dublin and met my future husband Damien, Joe felt that was going to be the end of me.

And Damien admits that for a time during the early years he was paranoid about the fact he wasn't an athlete. When I got injured and began to lose form, someone hinted to him that it was his fault and that his more relaxed lifestyle was now rubbing off on me. That of course was rubbish. When we began going out I won 20 races in a row, and I know that was largely down to this newfound happiness.

Damien eventually realised his lack of involvement in athletics wasn't so strange or unusual, even if many athletes do marry other athletes or sometimes their coaches. Besides, Damien had a big interest in athletics and became more and more knowledgeable as he travelled to more and more races with me. He also got to know people on the running scene. And I went to more dinners and award ceremonies, something I rarely did before I met him.

Joe knew how dedicated I was. I trusted him and he trusted me. I was always honest with him about the training I did, although I didn't always tell him about the little extra I might have done. I didn't need to. Like whenever he told me to run 45 minutes in the morning he just knew I'd go out and do 50 minutes. I'd always do that extra five or 10 minutes, never the other way around. If he said go out and do an easy 10-mile run I'd go out and do 12. I was just so driven that I felt I had to do a little more. To this day I've never once cut a run short unless I had to.

Even when the marathon came around he might tell me to do a two-and-a-half-hour run. Even that wasn't enough – I'd have to add on another five minutes. That's the way most of the successful runners are.

Obviously, if Joe was there with me I wouldn't be doing anything extra. When we got into the marathon training and started doing long tempo runs he would travel just behind me in the car, and those runs never went farther than they were supposed to.

But it wasn't like Joe ever needed to tell me to be in bed at a certain time. I knew that myself. We both had a simple and commonsense approach to a lot of things. The difference between despair and hope is a good night's sleep – that was one of his favourite sayings. If things weren't working out just go to bed and everything would be grand the next morning.

As time went on, the relationship became even more businesslike. Even before big races he would never get excited. But then there wasn't any need to hype me up or anything like that. He didn't believe in pep talks, because it was the hard work that mattered. All the success came down to the training, not to anything that was said.

There were days when we both knew I was unbeatable and nothing else needed to be said. Other days he might say you're as good as, if not better than, any of them. You have the winning of this.

It all came down to the sheer hard work of the training. He liked to get me to the stage where he knew I couldn't do anything more, not another mile or another stride. With that feeling I was generally unbeatable.

No more than my parents, he didn't like to brag about what I'd done. The only exception to that was after I won the London marathon in 1998, when I went up to his school to meet some of his students. That was quite nice and I enjoyed that. He'd never asked me to do anything like that before so I was glad to help out. And that day he did talk very highly of me, introducing me as this great runner. I got a lot of satisfaction hearing him say that.

Even after some of my biggest victories he would keep things under control. He would always keep things low-key. He'd prefer to go back to the hotel and just relax. But he would enjoy that sense of satisfaction, and I suppose the relief as well. He just hated bullshit and would never suffer a fool. He said it as it was and never really courted any publicity or popularity. If you didn't like it, tough luck.

The day after any major race it was straight back to business. It wasn't like we switched off and enjoyed ourselves for the next two weeks. But I had this problem after races. It sounds terrible but I could hardly remember anything afterwards. He'd be asking me about how I felt at halfway or wherever, or why I broke away when I did, but he just couldn't get it out of me.

I wouldn't be able to recall very much. I suppose I was in the zone or whatever you want to call it. I always thought that was a good thing. But I could never tell him how I felt at a certain stage because I honestly couldn't remember. And, understandably, he'd get a little frustrated with that.

CHAPTER 5
YOU'RE A BIG GIRL NOW

BRENDAN FOSTER ONCE SAID THAT LONG-DISTANCE RUNNERS that train hard feel tired all the time. They wake up tired, they go around all day feeling tired, and they go to bed tired. I suppose Foster should know. Like most of the great long-distance runners in England in the 1970s he trained very hard.

By the end of 1991 I was training very hard. I was running every day and sometimes twice a day as well as doing the bounding sessions specifically designed by Joe Doonan. I was also working full-time in the courthouse of Cavan County Council. But I very rarely felt tired. I woke up every day with the energy to go running and would generally be full of energy going to bed at night. I could have run three or four times a day if I really wanted to.

Even with my job, my whole daily routine was based around running. In so many ways I was giving it exactly the same commitment as any professional athlete would. I'd leave the house at nine in the morning to get into Cavan for work and would usually take a lift with my sister Eileen. She was working in town and her office happened to be directly across the road from the court-house where I worked.

My main training run of the day would take place at lunchtime, which at first meant one o'clock on the dot. The only problem was that everyone else was spilling out for lunch at the same time, and Farnham Street in Cavan would often be very busy. I was still way too shy to be seen running by so many people, so I'd come to a simple agreement with Eileen.

She would run out of her office and jump into her small car parked outside. She'd drive across the street and stop outside the courthouse, and I'd be there waiting for her – still in my working clothes, of course. I'd jump into the back seat, where that morning I'd laid out my running shorts and T-shirt.

We'd speed off out the road to Cavan golf course, which was about three minutes away, and I'd pull on the running gear as we drove. Once we got there I'd just jump out and start running straight away. I only had about 50 minutes to train, because at exactly 10 minutes to two Eileen would be back to collect me. I'd slip back into my uniform and head straight into work. Eileen was very good to endure that for as long as she did.

Even after I'd won my second national senior cross-county title, in 1991, and a couple more big races around the country I was still uselessly shy when it came to running down that street in Cavan. Eventually, and I don't know what got into me, I found the courage to run straight out to the golf course.

The other problem was that the golf course would often be very muddy, especially in the middle of winter. So I'd be arriving back to work with mud splattered all up my legs and arms, and sometimes even my face. All I could do was pull my tights up over my legs and try to scrub my face in the bathroom. There was no shower in the courthouse at the time.

Brian Johnston, the county manager at the time, started to let me out at 12.20 if I needed to do some special training session and told me to come back whenever I was finished. That meant a lot to me, but I never abused the privilege – all the time I was out of the office I spent running.

Mr Johnston, as I always called him, was a true supporter and a great inspiration. He was a big personality and had a raw sense of humour, but he was very warm. Over the years I became somewhat infamous on the athletics circuit for the huge support I brought with me. Up to 50 or 60 people would travel to my big races, and Mr Johnston organised a lot of those trips. It was always a mixed bunch – county councillors, local TDs, journalists, business people and neighbours too numerous to name.

Between them all there would always be one big party somewhere after my races. I can still hear Mr Johnston's loud laugh dominating these gatherings. I was devastated when he died suddenly playing golf in May 2003. He was a great boss, a great supporter and a great friend, and he played a huge role in helping me make it in athletics.

Going into the cross-country season of 1992, I only had one real goal, and that was the World Championships in Boston at the end of March. I had decided I was going to do whatever I could to get there in the best shape of my life. But this wasn't something I ever talked about with Joe. We never made plans like that. Joe just planned the training sessions week by week, and I would often get more uptight about them than I would about the races, especially when Joe was there watching me.

More often than not the racing was actually easier than the training. I'd done so much running on the hills that the flat races were definitely easier, and I knew going into those races that I was as fit as anyone could be.

I'd been making steady progress for the previous two years since running my first World Cross Country, in Stavanger in 1989. I'd won my second national title in February of 1991, which was again staged in Limerick, beating Ann Keenan Buckley by 50 seconds, one of the biggest winning margins ever.

I'd also had two full summers of running on the track, and while that wasn't always to my liking, it had definitely improved my leg speed and I could feel the difference.

I'd also had the experience of two further World Cross Country runs. On winning my first national title in 1990 I was selected to run in Aix-les-Bains, a small, picturesque town in the foothills of the French Alps. It was a particularly warm day at the end of March, even for that part of France, and the course was possibly the flattest cross-country course I'd ever run on. The pace, however, wasn't exceptionally fast. The American Lynn Jennings had pulled away by the end of the first lap and ended up winning by 12 seconds. She was 29 years old and that was her first world title – she had taken the silver medal behind Zola Budd back in 1986.

I went in there determined to improve on my 76th position of the year before. I went out a little harder, although I still wasn't totally comfortable with so many runners around me. You have to fight for every place in the World Cross Country but I held my form and finished in 40th position, 55 seconds behind Jennings. It wasn't the kind of result to make headlines back home and yet I knew it was another important breakthrough. I left Aix-les-Bains already looking forward to the following year.

The 1991 championships were set for a racecourse in Antwerp. I'd raced in Belgium a few times by then and figured it was probably the next-best thing to home territory. We had decided I should run in some of the bigger cross-country races in Europe, one of which was held annually in Acoteias, Portugal. I went over hoping to run well and ended up winning. I had no idea at the time but that race was also famous for the prize money, and I won something like £3,000. They paid that out in cash, hundreds of these escudo notes in this brown paper bag. I didn't know what to do with it.

I was flying out that evening and figured the best thing to do was stuff the notes into the pockets of my tracksuit. I got onto the plane with all my pockets bulging with money.

My brother Seán collected me at Dublin airport.

Well, how did you get on? He made it sound like I'd bet on a horse.

I started pulling notes out of various pockets and showed Seán the big bundle of money.

Janey, there must be a million pounds there, he said, laughing.

When we got home I just walked into the kitchen with the brown paper bag and emptied the cash onto the table. My father was sitting by the fire and just glanced over at it. Good lassie, he said, you did alright.

The money on the table meant nothing to me. Showing it off was purely a symbolic gesture, as if to say I was starting to look after myself now. That's what he was most satisfied about as well.

That victory did a lot for my confidence heading off to the World Cross Country in Antwerp. It rained a lot in the days leading up to the race, but the organisers spread sand in the wettest patches, and we were told it wouldn't be muddy. That sounded like good news to me. People thought because I was Irish I thrived in the muck, but I hated it.

Just when I thought everything was going to plan, I found myself going to bed that night feeling a bit off. I had the classic flu symptoms, feeling hot one minute and shivering the next. There's always the danger that when you hit peak fitness, when you've been training long and hard for several weeks like I had done, your immune system is more open to catching bugs, and that's exactly what happened to me. There's nothing you can do about it, and I certainly wasn't going to tell anyone but Joe.

Because of my good form through the season most of the Irish athletics journalists had travelled over, and I knew they expected something of me. I expected something too.

How about the top 20, Catherina? Ah, we'll see how it goes.

But at no point in that race did I feel like myself. I was out of it after the first lap and ended up in 65th place. Jennings retained her title, and this time I was over 90 seconds back. Not exactly the sort of progress I'd planned on making.

I didn't want to make a big deal about being sick, but I could see the disappointment in the eyes of everyone I met that day. It was the first small setback of my career but the disappointment of that race made me even more determined to train harder than ever. I knew myself that I just wasn't right that day, and I suppose I felt like I had something to prove. Sometimes a little pain and anger like that can bring even more out of you.

Joe was eager for me to get another good track season under my belt, and in June of 1991 I ran 8:57.5 for 3,000 metres, and that qualified me for the World Championships in Tokyo.

It was an unbelievably long trip and once again I still wasn't enjoying the atmosphere of the track, but the experience would stand to me. The only problem with that trip was it meant I'd miss Peadar's wedding. I was sorry to miss it, but Eileen was getting married a few months later so at least I could look forward to that.

The build-up to Boston began more or less as soon as I came home. Joe was already laying down a programme of races. That was also the first year the IAAF developed a World Cross Grand Challenge, which just like their Grand Prix series on the track allowed athletes collect points over various races. There were double points on offer at the World Cross Country, and that was added to your four best races over the season. Then they'd announce the overall winners, with £10,000 each for the best man and woman.

The first Grand Challenge race was set for Bolbec in France on December 1st. It was early in the season but a lot of the big names were there, such as Albertina Dias of Portugal, who was second in Aix-les-Bains, and Annette

Sergent of France, who had won in Stavanger. It just wasn't as crowded as the World Cross Country, and for that reason I was able to get right up to the front. I was never out of the top three or four, and in the end I beat them all. Dias was two seconds back, and from that day on I felt I could beat anyone.

I got a flight out of France that evening and was back in Cornafean by around 10 o'clock. I went straight to bed and slept sound in the knowledge that I'd be back at my desk at work in the morning.

Three weeks later, and just three days before Christmas, I was in Mol, in Belgium, for the second Grand Challenge race. I won that by four seconds.

After that I had nearly two weeks' holidays from work and was able to increase the training that little bit more. I trained every day as usual, but I was now able to train twice a day as well if I wanted to. And I could also enjoy Christmas.

One of the questions I've been asked most often is whether or not I trained on Christmas Day. Anybody who asks that question obviously hasn't a clue about distance running. Of course I trained on Christmas Day, and that also meant I didn't have to help get the dinner ready – I was running in the fields.

Around that time one of the best cross-country races in Europe took place in Mallusk, just outside Belfast, on the first Saturday in January. They've had nearly all the big names there over the years, and there would always be a big crowd coming up from south of the Border. My training had gone very well over the Christmas and I was definitely looking forward to another good run there.

About a week before the race it was announced that Sonia O'Sullivan would also be running. I had only heard bits and pieces about her since she'd gone to Villanova on scholarship, but she was already making a big name for herself. She'd hadn't competed in Tokyo with me because of injury, but she was coming to Belfast. This was probably her only chance to impress the Irish selectors because she was heading back to America a day or two later.

I didn't think about her at all going into that race because I was going to run to my own plan anyway, and that meant going hard from the gun. As it turned out, I never even saw Sonia in the race – she didn't really figure at the front. Just like in Bolbec and Mol, I timed my run well and won by four seconds from Lieve Siegers of Belgium.

Boston was still around 10 weeks away so I was careful not to overdo it. I didn't race again until February 9th, when I went back to Acoteias in Portugal and was just beaten by this particularly fast Ethiopian, Lucia Yishak.

No reason to panic. Two weeks later I won my third successive National cross-country over a fairly flat and fast course in Santry, this time by 52 seconds from Una English. I was flying that day, and all I had to do now was stay healthy. Joe and myself were more certain than ever that things were coming together, and suddenly anything was possible in Boston.

By then though, the whole of Cornafean had copped on to the fact I might do well in the World Championships. A few people got together and organised a raffle, the prize being two plane tickets to Boston to support me. They sold hundreds of tickets and held the draw in McSeáin's pub about a week before the race. And who should win it only my old friend Geraldine Mulligan, who was very well known around the area.

That caused great excitement until Geraldine realised she had no passport. To be honest, not many people around Cornafean had passports at the time.

There was now massive concern, and people seemed a lot more worried about how Geraldine would get there than about my prospects. I could have been lying in bed with a broken leg. All the talk was about how she could get her passport. Any word on Geraldine? That was the first thing people would say when they met on the road.

Everyone wanted her to go. As it turned out, another neighbour of ours was working at the American Embassy in Dublin. He managed to get the thing sorted out and that was a huge relief to everyone. And it probably even took a bit of pressure off me. Geraldine travelled out with her father, Tommy, and they had a great time.

Peadar had also arranged to travel over, and a few of the county councillors did too. But Joe had wisely arranged for himself and myself to travel out a full week before. The Irish team weren't due to travel until the Wednesday before the race, which didn't leave much time to recover from jet lag.

I had met John Treacy the previous summer, and he'd invited me to stay with him for the week before the race to help acclimatise. He said he had plenty of room, and he meant it. Joe and I flew into Boston the Sunday before, and John brought us straight down to his house in Providence, Rhode Island, less than an hour away. It was a lovely, big house in one of those wide, sprawling

American neighbourhoods. It was a fabulous place and I felt at home there straight away.

John had just won the Los Angeles marathon a few weeks before, revisiting the city of his Olympic silver medal eight years earlier, and he was just recovering after that, but we went for a few short runs around a nearby golf course.

On the Tuesday morning I did my usual blow-out, the last hard run before the race, on the same golf course, with Joe and John watching. I felt very good, and even John was impressed with the shape I was in.

The next day Joe realised he'd have to go back home because his mother was very, very sick. He had no choice. He left on the Thursday morning. The last thing he said to me was I was going to win a medal. That got me thinking very positively, and from then on I was sure I would get a medal.

Later that day it started snowing quite heavily, which was fairly normal for New England at that time of year. I had planned on doing a few strides after my run, but you couldn't really go out the door.

Luckily, John had a treadmill machine in his house, set up in his office. I was able to do an easy 30-minute run on that, which was better than not running at all because of the snow. John had a TV set up right next to it, so you could just stare at that. Then I told John I needed to do a few strides as well. He just looked at me and told me to forget about the strides. I was a bit upset about that, because I would always do whatever I'd planned, regardless of what happened. But of course at that stage it wasn't going to make any difference.

John's wife, Fionnuala, was very nice to me. She cooked a massive dinner that Thursday night, with loads and loads of potatoes. I'd also cooked one of my own loaves of brown bread for the week. My mother would always cook it at home, so I just brought over the ingredients and mixed it up myself. I don't know if it made any difference, but that was all part of the routine.

John had four beautiful young children and they were great company.

The race was on the Saturday, and all the teams were staying in the Boston Towers, a massive hotel in the heart of downtown Boston. John drove me up there on the Thursday evening, and I met up with the rest of the Irish team.

The following morning all the teams headed out to the course, which was a short distance away in Franklin Park, easily the biggest open space in Boston.

I'd never really felt the cold that much before, but I felt it that day. There was the odd snow flurry, with more forecast. We ran over parts of the course, which included a fairly tough hill known as the Bear Cage. The finish line was inside an old American football pitch known as the White Stadium. I felt it was a good course.

For the rest of the evening most of us just hung around the hotel lobby. I was in total awe of the place, it was so, so big. People were coming and going, but I was very, very relaxed, and just ready to go.

The day of the race itself was freezing cold. Looking out the window it looked clear and quite sunny, but outside you'd be hit with the odd shower of snow and a blast of icy wind. The Americans were going on about the wind-chill factor, and how that would make it so difficult to run. I didn't know what they were talking about. When we got to the course I spotted some Belgian runners, and they had rubbed black polish under their eyes, which reduces the reflection of the sun. I thought that was very strange.

Some of the other runners were wearing tights while warming up, which I hadn't seen much of before, and everyone was wearing gloves. I was happy to run around in my knicker-shorts and vest. And I didn't wear gloves. Even on the coldest days back home I would rarely wear anything else other than the shorts and T-shirt.

Although I was very relaxed at the start, you can't but get a little nervous. All the teams are lined up in individual pens, which stretch out for something like 100 metres. There's unbelievable tension for a few minutes as every runner gets ready for the best start possible. If you stopped to think about it for too long you'd be afraid to run at all.

I was standing at the front of the Irish pen along with Sonia. The rest of the team was Geraldine Hendricken, Monica O'Reilly, Teresa Duffy and Breeda Dennehy. We'd talked a little bit beforehand and believed we had an outside chance of a team medal if everyone ran well.

You don't just start running in the World Cross Country; you have to start charging. The first few hundred metres are flat out. I wasn't going to kill myself to get into a good position. I knew they'd start coming back to me after 800 metres or so. The race was 6.3 kilometres, about four miles, and there was plenty of time to make up ground.

One of the first things I learnt about racing was that if you go out too fast you will pay for it, and if you go out too slow you give yourself too much work to do. But I was naturally good at judging my pace. Normally as the race wore on I would feel better. That was something that also came naturally to me.

As usual it was one of the Kenyans who was leading, Susan Sirma. The leading bunch was a bit ahead of me for a while, but going into the second lap I was exactly where I wanted to be.

Then with about 5 kilometres run there were only three of us left. Albertina Dias was leading, with Lynn Jennings and myself running just behind her. My plan was to make one big move and try to break them.

I hit the front with about 900 metres to go. I got ahead of them quite easily but still didn't feel like I was running flat out. I knew the finish was getting closer and closer because more people were shouting with every stride. Come on, Catherina, you've got it. Or else come on USA.

I knew I'd gone a few strides clear, but for some reason I couldn't quite see myself winning. It wasn't so much that I didn't have the confidence to finish it off. It was more like I didn't have the confidence to take them on much earlier in the race and run away from them in the way I could have. Something was telling me that this was too big of an occasion to be leading. Like this is America I'm in, such a long, long way from Cornafean. You can't just run away from people here. I know that sounds stupid now but that's what I was thinking then. That's what you call inexperience.

Physically I felt like doing it, but mentally I just wasn't able. That was the experience I lacked, and that's what cost me the gold medal, and not what happened in the final 80 metres between Jennings and myself.

Coming into the finishing chute we were together again, and she made this huge surge. She had that extra bit of belief, nothing more. She'd won this twice before. She'd grown up in New England and Franklin Park was her own back yard. Jennings won by two seconds. Dias was only a second behind me.

I heard afterwards that Jennings said it was one of her easiest wins. I'm not so sure about that.

Within seconds of crossing the line I had a great feeling of shock and excitement. I really couldn't believe I'd finished that high up. At no stage in the race did I actually feel cold but after crossing the finish line I realised my hands were completely frozen. For a good hour or so afterwards the pain was unbelievable. That was the only problem I had. The rest of my body was fine.

People started running up to me and slapping me on the back. All I was concerned about was my hands. I'd never experienced pain like that. One of the race officials came up to me and said I'd have to go for a drugs test. She realised my hands were frozen and gave me her big padded gloves, which I still have at home somewhere.

Lots of people were coming up to me to say well done. One of them was Andrew Boylan, a local TD and chairman of Cavan County Council, who had managed to get into the finish area by telling them he was the President of Ireland. Peadar was another one to get in, and he was highly excited.

I was led into the testing area and ended up sitting beside Jennings. She didn't say much, and of course I wasn't one to start a conversation. She would finish third the following year but I never got to know her at all. As far as I know, not many people did. She more or less kept to herself.

It was only when I got out of there that I found out we'd come very close to team medals. Sonia had run a great race to finish seventh, and Geraldine Hendricken was well up there too in 31st. Monica O'Reilly was a little farther back in 63rd but we still ended up fourth best, behind Kenya, America and Ethiopia. It was the highest ever placing by an Irish women's team.

After the medal ceremony it all began to sink in, and I was delighted with the result. Peadar offered to go on a bit of a warm-down with me, and during the run he said to me this was going to change things. And he was right.

When we got back from that someone told me that my second-place finish was more than enough to win the Grand Challenge. At that time there wasn't any prize money for the World Cross Country, but my Grand Challenge win was worth £10,000. That was definitely a nice consolation for not winning the gold medal in Boston.

It was late in the afternoon by the time we got back to the hotel. It was time to call home. I knew my father and mother and the rest of the family would have been glued to the television and were dying to talk to me. My mother was still very excited and started talking about Brendan Foster's commentary on BBC. She said Brendan didn't have a clue who I was and could hardly even pronounce my name.

She was giving out as well about my father, that he'd been smoking like a trooper and in the end they could hardly see the television with the smoke. I was getting a great laugh out of this. She said everyone had expected me to fall back. Then she admitted that she got too nervous to even watch and had to go out the back yard to relax and say a quick prayer.

There was a big banquet for all the runners that night. I went down for a half an hour or so, but after that all I wanted to do was go to bed. I had just won a silver medal in the World Cross Country, and £10,000 for being the most consistent runner all season, and I was in bed by 10 o'clock. I didn't even have a whiff of a drink that night. It just wasn't my style.

Because I'd come out on a different flight from the team I went home on a different one too. I slept nearly all the way, which was normal for me. Just before we landed in Dublin they announced that Catherina McKiernan was on board and had just won the silver medal at the World Cross Country.

There was a big crowd at the airport. The whole family had come down and I realised then what Peadar was talking about. Things were about to change. We left there and on to this big reception at Whitegate, which is on the Cavan-Meath border. There was a huge crowd of county councillors and various sporting officials. The family were there too, and someone said that Boston had brought me out of Cornafean and into every household in Ireland.

Boston did change the way people saw me and also my running career, but it didn't change the way I felt about running. It definitely raised expectations a lot more, and the pressure that came with that. From that day on, every time I went out in a cross-country race people expected me to win, or at least to finish near the front. From that point of view things were never the same again. But it also gave me more confidence. Other than that the race never changed me, or the reasons I ran. I still enjoyed it as much, at least for the next few years.

The real homecoming was in McSeáin's pub and was organised by the GAA club. The place was packed and I sat there and listened to all these people saying great things about me, and I was grateful for everything they said. But as you can imagine, I was a little bit uncomfortable with all the praise. I was just one of the locals everyone knew, just one of their neighbours. It was lovely to be treated like that by my neighbours, but I never felt different from anyone else.

A few years later I watched a video of that night and couldn't believe what I was seeing. There I was with these big, rosy cheeks in a funny outfit and an awful-looking hairdo. All I could do was stand there, hands behind my back, staring at the floor. But looking back it was a great occasion.

Boston opened up a lot of sponsorship opportunities and I was more than happy to let Peadar look after that end of things. In doing so he effectively became my manager. I knew he was someone I could trust and I know he did his best for me over the years.

On the Tuesday I was back at work, and my boss, Brian Johnston, was so delighted he offered to get a shower installed in the council offices so I'd be able to wash off after my training runs at lunchtime.

At first he said he'd got someone to sponsor it, and all they wanted in return was a publicity photograph of me using the shower after a training run. It was no big deal, he said. We'd make sure it was well steamed up before we let the photographer in. I didn't realise he was only having me on. He was always joking around like that. Despite what happened in Boston, it hadn't changed me a bit.

CHAPTER 6
FOURTH TIME AROUND

HAVING COME WITHIN TWO OR THREE STRIDES OF WINNING the World Cross Country in 1992 I was faced with two options going into the new season. I could try out new training methods, start raising the bar a little higher, perhaps even adapt the full-time approach in my quest to go one place better next time. Or I could continue very much as before.

Of course the first scenario wasn't going to happen. I really only had one option, and that was to stick to the only routine I knew. I couldn't have broken out of that even if I wanted to. I was perfectly content to go into Cavan County Council every morning. I was probably attracting a little more attention than the average receptionist but that didn't bother me. I liked the atmosphere and the mood of the place. You could only do so much running in one day, and I didn't want to be sitting at home the rest of the time twiddling my thumbs.

So approaching the World Cross Country of 1993 I was doing the same sort of training, repeating a lot of the hill sessions on the golf course and more or less running the same races.

I finished third in the first Grand Challenge race of the year, in Bolbec, France, but came out three weeks later and won in Mol. I also won again in Mallusk, and after that I decided to race in Seville. And I won that one too.

Obviously things were going exactly to plan.

The National cross-country was staged in the Phoenix Park in Dublin, and I won my fourth consecutive title without any problem. Ann Keenan Buckley from Laois finished second again, and I had to feel a little sorry for her. It was her fourth silver medal. How cruel that must be, I thought. In fact Ann won two more silver medals, in 1995 and 1996, before winning her first national title in 2000 – aged 38.

Joe was so sure I'd win in the Phoenix Park that he didn't travel down. Instead he went on an exploratory mission to Amorebieta, in the north of Spain, the venue for the World Cross Country on March 28th.

It's not a cross-country course at all, he said. It's as flat as a runway and the pace is going to be fast and furious. At least we knew what exactly was coming, and so we made the necessary adjustments in training.

We also decided to travel over a day ahead of the Irish team, again just to give me the extra bit of time to acclimatise. Not surprisingly, it was quite warm when we got there, about 20 degrees, and definitely a little more humid than it had been back home

A press conference was organised for the Friday afternoon with some of the fancied runners, and I was asked to attend. As usual I found it easy to say no and didn't need Joe's encouragement to stay away.

It was the first time South Africa had sent a team to the championships since the end of apartheid. And they had a few contenders in the women's race, including Zola Pieterse, better known as Zola Budd. She had won two titles for England in the 1980s but was now back running for her native country. She wasn't quite the skinny young girl I remembered but she was running well again.

Elana Meyer was also there for South Africa, having won the 10,000-metre silver medal in the 1992 Olympics behind Derartu Tulu of Ethiopia. They gave the press plenty to write about. My seat at the table was left empty.

Most of the newly independent countries of Eastern Europe were also there, competing individually for the first time, such as Russia, the Czech Republic, Belarus and Latvia, and the field of 149 runners was the largest yet.

As far as Portugal were concerned, Albertina Dias was the big favourite. And she was running very well. I had beaten her a couple of times during the season, but this was clearly the race she was gearing for all along.

The course itself had been the venue for the Zornotza cross-country for 32 years and was ridiculously flat. The highest climb was only three metres. They'd laid down man-made obstacles to make it a little more testing, and they gave them names too, such as Shrubb and Yifter, after the famous runners. The only thing I was familiar with was the distance – 6.35 kilometres.

Pieterse took the lead early, which was more or less the only way she knew how to run. I was happy to sit back off the leaders for a while. At around three kilometres Meyer took it up. Also somewhere around there, Tulu dropped out with a knee injury.

There were a fierce number of good runners in that field, and it was a much, much harder race than Boston. Jennings was back looking for a fourth title, and Liz McColgan of Scotland seemed to be back running at her best. On top of all that the Kenyan women were starting to match the Kenyan men in terms of depth and talent. They were all there.

At one stage Meyer seemed to get away, but I was able to latch right onto her. But so was Dias. That left the three of us running together at the front. We had opened a small gap on the rest and we made sure the pace never let up.

Dias was leading the charge now and ran the fifth kilometre in 3:15. I was still right on her heels, feeling okay but not quite able to push that kind of pace any faster. Dias ran the next kilometre quicker again, in 3:08, and with that she opened a 25-metre lead. She was able to stay ahead to the finish and won by nine seconds in 20 minutes even.

I was definitely tiring coming to the finish. I took one glance behind and saw Jennings flying up behind me. There was no way in hell she was going to beat me again, and I held her off for second. We were both timed at 20:09.

Pieterse was fourth in 20:10, and McColgan fifth in 20:17. It was the closest finish in a long time. And definitely the fastest women's cross-country race anyone could remember.

I was delighted to cross that line in second place. It was as tough a race as I'd ever run, and I certainly wasn't disappointed that I didn't win it. Getting another silver medal was a total relief. Straight away I realised people were going to think second again, but I was very, very happy with that.

The truth is I held on for that silver medal. The pace was smoking all the way from the gun, and it was a great feeling just to be able to mix it with them, the very best in the world. That gave me great satisfaction.

A large group of Irish supporters had travelled over, and while they were disappointed I didn't win, they realised just how difficult the race had been and were thrilled as well. Brian Johnston had organised a trip for a lot of the Cavan county councillors and various officials.

One of the group was the late Brian Finlay, another great supporter of mine over the years. The night before the race, he had a few extra beers and ended up sleeping in the next morning and missing the bus to the race. He was unbelievably apologetic that evening – embarrassed and mad at himself for coming all the way to Spain and missing the race. Brian, I said, I would have won it if you were there.

Joe was well pleased with the way things had gone. He knew all the best runners in the world were there, and it was a great achievement to come away with a medal. He said a few times that I'd run as well as I could have, and Dias was just that little bit better on the day. It was the highlight of her career. She'd won bronze in Boston and silver in 1990, so she had the complete set of medals.

Even coming away from Spain I didn't have any feelings of regret – or the sense that I'd definitely have to come back next year and win it. It was probably the hardest race I'd ever run and I was totally satisfied with the way I'd handled it. I'd also won my second Grand Challenge and collected another £10,000.

It was on the flight home that I first got talking to Paula Radcliffe. She had won the junior women's race in Boston, which was a brilliant achievement.

Over the next few years I got to know Paula probably better than I did any other runner. We talked quite a bit whenever we crossed paths and she was always very friendly to me. If Paula had any bit of news at all about the course or what time the buses were leaving or something like that she'd always make sure you knew about it. It was obvious she was always very determined about her own career and I admired that.

Back home the reaction to my silver medal was again fantastic. I just wanted to get back to work and my own routine, but there was the now customary awards ceremony in McSeáin's. I loved to see other people celebrating on my behalf, especially my family. I was happy to leave them singing and drinking on into the night while I slipped off home and went to bed.

Amorebieta also reinforced my belief that my training and racing routines were bringing out the best in me. There was still no reason to change anything around for the new season, and I didn't. I did take a few weeks off work that autumn to help rest up for the harder training, but it didn't feel like very long before the 1994 cross-country season was under way.

Bolbec was again the first big race of the season, and it was no surprise that Dias showed up. We had another great battle that day, but this time I got to the line first.

Mallusk was another customary stop off, and a huge crowd travelled up from Cavan that day. By then our neighbour Packie-Joe McGlade would make a regular run up, filling his bus on a first-come-first-served basis. The only notice he ever put out was via the local priest in Coronea, Fr John Phair, who at 10 o'clock Mass the Sunday before Mallusk would invite anyone interested in going to Catherina's race in Belfast to contact Packie-Joe. And now we'll say a Hail Mary that she does well, he would add. And the whole church would break into that with great enthusiasm.

I'll never forget the crowd of locals that used to show up in Mallusk. The McSeáins, the McGibneys, the Martins, all the O'Reillys, the Sheridans, George Cartwright, Phil Miney, the Gormleys, the Cullens, the Mulligans, Seán Masterson and the Duignans. And dozens more neighbours and friends from Cornafean.

I was in the middle of hard training going to Mallusk that year but I still expected to win. What I didn't expect was that Paula Radcliffe would take off at such a scorching pace. But she'd been steadily improving since winning the junior title in Boston, and she just about managed to stay ahead of me in Mallusk.

After the race I was interviewed for television and I was trying to apologise for not winning, thinking everyone at home would be watching. I didn't realise it was going out on BBC, and there I was apologising for not beating a British runner. I suspect that didn't go down too well in parts of Northern Ireland.

After winning again in Seville, the plan was to run the Acoteias cross-country again in Portugal, stay there to train in the Algarve sunshine for a week, and then head to Luxembourg for one last race before the World Cross Country, which in 1994 was destined for Budapest in Hungary.

The organisers in Acoteias typically offered two plane tickets over, so I persuaded my mother to come with me for the week. Joe was coming too but I would be glad of the extra company. She'd never been on an aeroplane before.

When we left Heathrow in London on the Thursday it was freezing, around minus four, and the Friday morning in the Algarve it was 20 degrees. My mother thought she was in heaven.

We decided to walk down to the course, about 15 minutes from the apartment. I was quite familiar with the place, having been there three times before. But this was great excitement, and my mother got all dressed up to go and carried a new handbag under her arm. We got down to the course and I did about half an hour running around while she walked around in the warm sunshine, looking at flowers. She loves gardening.

Heading back to the apartment we passed through an area where they were doing a lot of building work. As we walked down a narrow little road two guys came flying along on a motorbike, and the guy on the back snatched my mother's bag right from under her arm.

At least there wasn't much in the handbag. A little money obviously, but the only really valuable thing was her glasses. So she was without them for the week.

All she could do was laugh about it, but I was raging. We explained at the reception what happened. They were quite sympathetic and called the police, but sure we never heard any more. That just made me more determined to win the race the next day, which I did.

Thankfully, that didn't put my mother off the travelling. She came with me to a few races after that in France and Belgium.

As it turned out, the bag-snatching incident wasn't the worst thing to happen in Acoteias. It was so nice and warm in Portugal that I was doing most of my running in T-shirts and shorts, and from there I went into freezing cold and wet in Luxembourg. I'd never experienced such cold and damp. And of course I picked up a bit of a bug after the race.

I missed about four or five days of training, which wasn't too bad. But the body needs that time again to fully recover, so I wasn't really firing on all cylinders for about two weeks. That meant I was going into the World Cross Country having been knocked off course a little for the first time. Before Boston and Amorebieta everything had gone exactly to plan. This time I was going to Budapest with a slight doubt in my mind.

The championships were staged at the old Kincsem Park racecourse. The weather wasn't bad, cool but quite windy. Again I'd gone out a few days before the team, just to make sure I was totally settled into the place and well familiar with the course.

The race set off at noon, this time three laps of around two kilometres – and it started raining just as we got going. The field wasn't quite as stacked as the year before, but there was lots of talk about the Chinese runners, who had effectively come out of nowhere to smash all these world records on the track the summer before. At least some of the athletes that had won all those medals at the World Championships in Stuttgart were there.

The pace was quite slow for the first lap or so, but even still I was well down the field. I just didn't have the confidence to run hard with the leaders the whole way. The plan was to keep as much as I could in reserve and come through as best I could on the last lap or so. There were more of these man-made obstacles, including several logs. One of them was so big that they agreed to cut it away before the race after several runners had failed to clear it during practice the day before. It was ridiculously high.

Up front I could see they weren't running that hard. Zola Pieterse again took the lead early on, but going into the second lap, a couple of the Kenyans started pulling away. I didn't recognise either of them and wasn't too concerned about having to go with them. No one else was either.

By around halfway one of the Kenyans still had a clear advantage on the chasing bunch, which included myself, Dias and another Portuguese runner, Conceicao Ferreira. It was around that stage too that I first heard the name Hellen Chepngeno on the announcer's loudspeaker.

There was a sharp turn entering the final straight after each lap, and I could see Chepngeno's lead was down to 20 metres as we entered the last lap. She seemed to surge again and was soon 50 metres in front again. Dias was second, and I'd pulled myself up to third, about 40 metres back. I also had Ferreira and Elana Meyer for company. But I realised then I was in the position again to win.

Ferreira then got up to pass Dias, and that seemed to demoralise Dias, which worked to my advantage. Coming into the finishing straight I got past Ferreira. I sprinted flat to the boards but Chepngeno was still too far ahead. She won in 20:45 – seven seconds ahead of me, with Ferreira just a stride behind me in third. The Ethiopian Merima Denboba surged again for fourth, and Dias dropped back to fifth.

I'd never really run a race like that before, where I'd come from such a long way back. All around the last lap I felt I was catching them and catching them. I just wasn't feeling as good as the previous two years and wasn't able to get to the front the way I normally would.

But because of all this I was delighted again with that silver medal. I hadn't panicked at any stage; I just ran my own race and kept working away. The first thing I did when I crossed the line was to bless myself and thank God for getting me through that one. I knew in my heart it could have gone disastrously wrong.

It was such a relief to get another medal, much more so than the year before. I'd never really expected it because of the training I'd missed.

Shortly after the finish I spotted Peadar and he had his fist raised. And I did the same. We both knew things were looking a little dodgy going into that race. Winning another medal was a real thrill. It also meant I'd scored enough points to win the World Cross Challenge for the third year in a row. Overall then not a bad day's work.

Of course some people were thinking I should have beaten Chepngeno, who was more or less unknown. She was definitely a surprise winner but the Kenyans are always capable of doing that on any given day. She had an interesting background, starting out in the high jump, and trained with the Kenyan Prison Services team, where she was a corporal. But she was well down the field a year later and wasn't heard of very much after that.

So I left with another silver medal around my neck, and I was delighted. For me it had been a hugely satisfying result after a very hard race. Of course I didn't realise I'd have to run harder still to win another medal a year later.

The obvious question people would ask about my three silver medals in succession was whether or not I would exchange them all for one gold. I could never get my head around that idea. Of course winning a gold medal would be nice, but I knew how hard I'd run to win the three medals, and I was delighted every time to win them.

But I was still only 24. The 1995 World Cross Country was coming to Durham, in the North of England, just across the water really. There was no reason why I couldn't turn silver into gold in 1995 – or even one of the years after that.

A couple of things had changed in my approach to training going into the 1994-1995 cross-country season. I'd taken a leave of absence from work, originally for six weeks after Budapest, as Joe had decided to try out altitude training for the first time. I returned to work for a short while after that but then decided on taking a longer leave of absence. It was left open-ended by Cavan County Council but this time I never actually went back.

A European cross-country championship was also being staged for the first time, set for Northumberland, England, on December 10th. That effectively meant peaking a lot earlier than I was used to. As usual Joe just planned the training back from that race, and it went very much to plan.

As it turned out, it was a very tough course and very windy, and I was neck and neck with Spain's Julia Vaquero coming into the home straight. It had been a hard battle all the way, and as I pushed for the line, I caught Julia with a couple of elbows and I think that helped to keep her back – I wasn't coming second again. I just about beat her to the line and became the first ever European Cross Country champion.

We planned another spell of altitude training after that, in the build-up to Durham. Joe was fond of the small city of Albuquerque in New Mexico. We'd be away for four weeks this time, the longest time I was ever away from home, and I was a little bit anxious about that.

As it happened, the weather turned harsh at home at the start of 1995 so it was good to get away from that. All I did was train, eat and sleep. I had my own apartment so I had to shop and cook for myself, and that took up the rest of the time. I had a couple of Danielle Steele novels as well for company.

But still I didn't really enjoy being away from home. Not even the excitement of being in America did anything for me. At least the training went very well, and we arrived home exactly three weeks before the 1995 World Cross Country.

I'd raced a little more sparingly over the winter, and in fact I hadn't raced since just before I left for Albuquerque, which by now was over six weeks ago. That was in Tourcoing, France, and the young Romanian Gabriela Szabo had beaten me in a sprint finish. That wasn't a major setback, because it was a dry and flat course, and she was preparing for the indoors. But she was also down to run in Durham, and most people thought she would be the one to watch.

The thing about Durham was that it was just 17 miles from Gateshead and so easily accessible to anyone who wanted to travel from Ireland. And of course they travelled in huge numbers. I think half of Cavan must have been there that day. Certainly most of my family and friends were. Even club runners from all over the country had made the trip. Someone had brought this huge banner – COME ON CATHERINA. You couldn't miss it.

I might have been lacking a little bit of sharpness because I hadn't raced in so long. But I knew I was as fit as I'd ever been and was quietly confident going into the race. I did my usual run over the course the day before, and after that I'd arranged to meet some of the Irish journalists, like Tom O'Riordan, Brendan Mooney, Peter Byrne, Greg Allen and Frank Greally. Just as I started talking to them Szabo walked right past me. I said hello and shook hands with her. Even though she'd beaten me in France I didn't really think she would figure.

The race was down for the Saturday, March 25th. By the time I got out to the course that morning there were already a huge number of Irish flags flying about. That definitely got the adrenaline going. Support like that affects different athletes in different ways but it always got me excited and more determined. I hated to think I would disappoint anyone who had come all the way over.

I was also well familiar with Durham, having run the Grand Challenge race over the same course earlier in the year, finishing second to one of the Kenyans. That day it was run in a pure mudbath, so we all expected another soft, soggy course again in March. But after a few dry weeks it was a completely different surface, fast and well suited to the Africans. And it suited me too, because I much preferred the firm surface to running in mud.

In many ways the stage was perfectly set for a gold-medal run. There was a huge Irish crowd there, and apart from Paula Radcliffe, there were no British contenders, so I suppose I had some local support also. And I knew I was running well, and I definitely had as much experience as anyone else in the race. So at 2.30 we set off to cover the 6.4 kilometres over three laps. It was almost totally flat except for a small hill shortly after the start of each lap.

As usual one of the Kenyans went straight to the front – Rose Cheruiyot, a real youngster. The pace was steady but nothing too severe. About six of us settled at the front after the first lap – myself, Derartu Tulu and Gete Wami of Ethiopia, as well as Paula Radcliffe and the other Kenyan, Sally Barsosio. The lead changed a few times, but I was always in control and feeling very confident. By now the crowd were totally behind me. For a second or two the idea did enter my mind that I was going to win this race at last.

Throughout the whole race the noise and the atmosphere were just unbelievable. There was also huge Ethiopian support there.

I'd decided to make my move going into the last lap, and so I put the head down and strode out at full flight. This left everyone behind, expect for Tulu. She just strode along beside me and then made her move going up the slight climb. Once she got away from me I knew she was gone.

Every time Tulu sped past the crowds you'd hear them roar for her, and then the shouts for me. That was incredible. Tulu was simply flying that day. I don't think anyone would have beaten her. I was as confident as I could have been and ran as well as I could – she was just better than me on the day. No athlete minds being beaten by someone they know is just that bit ahead of them on the day. There's absolutely no shame in that.

Tulu had dropped out in 1993 and was injured in 1994, and she had been second way back in 1991. This was her sixth attempt. She finished eight seconds ahead of me, and I was another 10 seconds ahead of Barsosio, who just held off another Kenyan, Margaret Ngotho, for third. As I expected, Szabo never really featured and ended up 10th.

My first feeling when crossing the line was a mixture of joy and relief, just like it had been in Boston, Amorebieta and Budapest. It didn't strike me in any way that here was another silver medal. I was delighted with that. The one thing athletes fear most is that they will run badly, well below expectations, and without exerting themselves to the limit.

I knew I had given it my all. I wasn't going to beat Tulu and no one else was either. She's proven herself many times as one of the greatest distance runners of all time, a true champion. She won another Olympic 10,000 metres title in Sydney, and then bronze in Athens. Tulu is the kind of athlete who comes along once in a generation. She is probably the best distance runner I have ever seen.

What made Tulu's victory even more impressive that day was that she'd endured a horrendous trip to Durham. The whole Ethiopian team ran into all sorts of difficulties getting there. They had to sleep on the floor of the airport and eventually had to travel through the night by bus. I'd heard that story just before the race and remember thinking Tulu must be tired.

We spoke quite a few times over the years. Her English wasn't very good, but she would always have a friendly smile and call me McKiernan. Ethiopians don't seem to call people by their first names.

To me there was nothing to be disappointed about. People thought I must have been fed up at finishing second again, but to me that's a success, not a failure. I did start to wonder though if I was ever going to win the thing. Deep down I suppose I still believed that some day it would happen for me.

Whenever I think about those four silver medals now, Boston always comes to mind first. It was the one race I think I probably could have won. It came the easiest to me, and physically it was well within my range. I just lacked the necessary experience to go the extra yard and win.

Amorebieta was just a case of being beaten by a slightly faster runner on a very fast course. I'll always remember the fast pace there. And I wasn't 100 per cent for Budapest. Then I met Tulu at her best. If she hadn't been there that day I would have run away with it. I know I would. I also came away from Durham with a fourth successive Grand Challenge title. I suppose in terms of consistency I was the best cross-country runner in the world.

It didn't quite become my mission in life but I was still driven to give the World Cross Country at least a couple more efforts. The 1996 championships had the added challenge of being staged in Cape Town in South Africa, and that meant travelling out a week in advance.

I headed out to the course on the Tuesday and did a few hills. Something didn't feel right, and Joe told the team doctor on the Thursday that I wasn't feeling good. My temperature was well up. The doctor just told me to take hot and cold showers because, with drug testing in mind, I had to be careful what medicine I took so close to competition.

Damien whom I had met for the first time a year earlier in Durham was one of the very few Irish journalists to travel to Cape Town. I didn't know him that well at all at the time but he arrived at my hotel in search of an interview. I was just going out for an easy run and clearly wasn't in great form. I just didn't want to talk to anyone and have to tell lies, because I wasn't about to announce to anyone that I had this slight sickness. That night Damien interviewed Peadar and Joe and a few others of the Irish travelling party. Thankfully, he didn't mind the fact that I didn't talk to him. Anyway, he managed to get a short interview with Nelson Mandela on the day of the race which made his trip.

John Downes of the Irish men's team had gone down with the same bug. When I woke up on the morning of the race I had a big cold sore on my lip, and I knew that wasn't a good sign.

The race was very fast up front. After the first lap Derartu Tulu was badly spiked. She lost a shoe after about 250 metres but got back up to finish fourth. Ethiopia still won the title, Gete Wami biding her time until midway through the last lap and winning in 20:12.

I felt drained during the whole race and was never in it. I ran 20:57 and finished 13th, and it was a hard day's work. I was very disappointed. I would gladly have taken another silver medal. Inside I knew I wasn't 100 per cent but it was still a hard place to finish.

I met Paula Radcliffe in the athletes' tent shortly afterwards. She'd been injured a few weeks earlier and could only manage 19th. So we kind of consoled each other a little bit. I could see she was very disappointed too.

A year later I went to the 1997 championships in Turin with an even greater handicap than a dose of flu. At the start of the season I was feeling a dull pain in my left Achilles tendon, and within a few weeks I couldn't run. It was the first serious injury of my career. I ended up trying to do sessions in the swimming pool, which straight away I didn't like.

After a few anxious weeks over Christmas I was finally ready to race at the start of the year and finished a good second in Belgium to the Romanian Elena Fidatof. We went back to Albuquerque for a fourth time, and while out there I won a 10-kilometre road race in Dallas in 31:32. Nothing wrong with that.

Still, coming into Turin I knew I just wasn't as sharp as I needed to be. When you miss a few weeks like that you're always playing catch-up in training. In a way Turin came around too soon.

The event itself was spectacular. The course was in the Valentino Park, in the heart of the city, and included these specially laid carpets of turf, which turned out to be great to run on. Sonia O'Sullivan was also on the Irish team and she led for most of the first lap. Then I took up the running and shared the lead for a while with Sally Barsosio.

I just didn't feel like I was running as strongly as I was the previous years. The pace never really felt comfortable. The fact that I'd missed so many races over the New Year period with injury really came against me that day. But I was still there going into the start of the last lap, along with five others, with Paula starting to make her move. She was obviously feeling good and came desperately close to winning. But Tulu swept past her in the last few strides.

I was still reasonably happy to finish seventh. It never felt like a race I was going to win. Tulu was at her best again, and Paula finished one second ahead of Gete Wami. Sonia was a couple of places behind me in ninth, five seconds back.

Turin was the first year they started handing out prize money – $40,000 for the winner, $30,000 for second, and so on down to sixth place, which got $5000. So I got nothing. Pity they didn't start that a few years before.

Then the team result was announced, and we'd finished third behind Ethiopia and Kenya. That was the first time the Irish women's team had won medals and that was definitely a big thrill. The team was myself and Sonia, Valerie Vaughan, Una English, Maureen Harrington and Pauline Curley.

When I arrived home though I did notice the hype was gone. There was nothing like the welcome-home parties of before. That was fair enough, but that made me feel a little bit more disappointed, like as if I had failed out there.

I didn't quite realise it at the time but that would be my last World Cross Country until 2004. But I knew I needed to change something and that I just couldn't keep on going into another season. Something had to break it up. I'd been doing more or less the same thing for eight years, and it had become too regimented, too predictable.

But I knew I could look back without regrets. I'd only had a handful of bad runs all through those years, and the happy days far outnumbered the not-so-happy ones. And I've got five World Championship medals – four individual and one team – to prove it.

I know I'll always be asked would I swap those four silvers for one gold. The answer is a definite no. To me winning four silver medals is a better achievement than winning one gold. Sure you could say it's unique.

CHAPTER 7
TOO MUCH OF NOTHING

I WILL PROBABLY BE REMEMBERED MOST FOR MY ENDEAVOURS in cross country and in the marathon. But looking back I did have a decent track career.

I've run in two Olympics Games on the track, two world championships, and once in the European championships. I've won five Irish titles on the track. I held the Irish 10,000-metre record for five years. And I've served my time on the Grand Prix circuit, from Osaka to Oslo and from Brussels to Berlin.

That's a lot of track races and the truth is I have a very good record despite the general opinion that I never did much on the track. When I trace the trail, I'd like to think I gave myself every chance of achieving the sort of satisfaction on the track that would have mirrored my satisfaction in cross-country.

But I also know that some of the things that made me so successful in cross-country also limited my success on the track. I tried to combine the two as best as I could but they ended up running parallel, with one always beyond the reach of the other.

One of my earliest memories of the track, and the race that probably set the mood for my entire track career, was the Irish Schools 3,000 metres in 1988, just a couple of months after I'd won the Schools cross-country title in Dungarvan.

I'd run away from everyone in Dungarvan without even trying too hard. I arrived at the track in Belfield expecting to do the same. I hit the front and led for lap after lap, but coming into the last 100 metres there was still someone running just behind me. It was Máiréad Looney from Cork, one of the girls I'd beaten in Dungarvan – she was second there. But in Belfield she sprinted past me, and there was nothing I could do about it.

I can think of so many races where exactly the same thing happened. I would usually end up leading nearly the whole race, and then people would start passing me on the last lap, sometimes one by one, until I finished fifth or sixth. That was not very enjoyable. In fact it would drive me mad.

I always knew from playing camogie that speed wasn't my strength. I could run and run around that field all afternoon, but I didn't have that turn of speed if another player suddenly broke away from me. I had to let her go. That sheer speed of the track specialists just killed me. Like when runners get up on their toes and really start motoring. I just wasn't made for those short, sudden bursts of speed.

Of course I worked on it, especially with the bounding drills designed to improve my sprinting style. I also did sessions along the lines of 20 times 400 metres. Sometimes I would finish off a session with some pure speedwork, such as 60-metre turnabouts – which meant exactly that. You run 60 metres as fast as you can, then turn around and do it again. That helped improve my speed to a certain extent but it wasn't going to turn me into a world-class 1,500-metre runner.

Later on, when I got more detailed physiological testing done in Trinity College, it became clear I was never going to develop that sheer speed, no matter how hard I worked on it. My muscles were made up primarily of slow-twitch fibres, with fewer fast-twitch fibres. That wasn't necessarily an insurmountable handicap, and it did mean I would run one hell of a marathon.

A runner like Paula Radcliffe has a similar make-up in that she doesn't have the pure turn of speed that someone like Derartu Tulu has. We've seen that enough times on the track. But then Paula developed the ability to run at a sustained pace a lot better than most other athletes on the track. She just got herself in front and gradually wore down the other runners to the point that no matter how fast they were, they weren't going to beat her.

That was the way I had to approach my track races. But finishing speed wasn't my only problem with the track. I also didn't like that feeling of confinement. I loved the freedom of cross-country, where I could stride out in front, or even hold back a little off the front, just to get the feeling of space. The track definitely didn't come as natural to me as the cross-country did.

I remember watching one of the track races at the Athens Olympics in 2004 with my daughter, Deirbhile, and after a while she just looked at me and asked: Where are they running to? I had to laugh at that, because that's the way I would feel sometimes running around the track. At least on a cross-country course I felt like I was going somewhere.

Another problem I had with the track season was the fact that I was always going into it after a hard cross-country season. If you look at any athlete that was really successful on the track, I don't think any of them came in with the same intensity of a cross-country season that I had. I would typically start racing sometime in November, right through until the end of March. That was five hard months of intense training and racing – not ideal preparation for the track. The fact is the pure track specialists would not have been racing nearly as much during that time.

So I always felt more and more tired as the track season wore on. The first couple of races I was usually quite sharp and often ended up running quite well. But when the really important races came around I was starting to feel a little stale. I was feeling more and more tired training, and a lot of the time I was just thinking about having a break. I would have to put a part of it down to the hard cross-country seasons one after another.

Say for some reason I'd missed a whole cross-country season, then it would have been interesting to see how the track season went. I said that to Joe one time, just asked him straight up if he thought I shouldn't concentrate so much on the cross-country. But we were too successful and enjoying it too much not to. I suppose I couldn't have it every way.

I won my first Irish senior title on the track as a 20-year-old in 1990, when I ran 9:16.60 to win the 3,000 metres in Tullamore. The year after that I won again in 9:10.93, and a few weeks later I lowered my best to 8:54.61, which was well inside the qualifying time for the World Championships in Tokyo. Joe believed it was well worth going for the experience, even though we both knew

I was going to be a little bit out of my depth.

It was an incredible trip and I didn't run too badly either, finishing sixth in my heat in just over nine minutes, and just two places short of making the final.

After I won the silver medal in the World Cross Country in 1992 it was automatically assumed I would make it to the Olympic Games in Barcelona that summer. The 3,000-metre qualifying time was nine minutes flat, and I had to chase it down a few times. I eventually ran 8:51.33 at the Helsinki Grand Prix, thanks in part to my new American rival Lynn Jennings, who won that night too.

It was a big thing, definitely, to qualify. More than anything else I was thrilled for the family and all my relations, the fact that they could talk about me going to the Olympics. People were talking about me being the first Cavan person to go to the Olympics. I would just laugh about it and tell them I'd probably be the last.

The truth is it just wasn't a big ambition of mine. It wasn't like I dreamed about the Olympics as a youngster growing up in Cornafean, or wrote the words Olympics 1992 above my bed or some place like that. I know most runners will tell you competing in the Olympics, and winning the Olympics, is one of the things they wanted to do from a very young age. To me the Olympics were more or less another race. I know it's easy to say that now but I never felt like the Olympics were somehow going to make or break my running career.

What I would say though is that the 1992 Olympics in Barcelona was a great experience, not just in terms of the running. There was so much hype about going that the whole experience started even before you got there, and I did enjoy a lot of that.

We went to a training camp beforehand down in the south of France. That was the first time I got to know Noel Berkeley, who was running in the 10,000 metres. He had this long, curly hair, which even back in 1992 seemed a little unfashionable. He really made me laugh, He used to shave his legs, and I'd never heard of a guy shaving his legs before. Definitely not around Cornafean. Even if they did, it wasn't something they would tell you about.

Even when we got into the athletes' village in Barcelona I never felt much pressure. I knew the whole thing was just a stepping stone to the future. No one expected me to do anything, and I knew myself I wasn't going to do anything.

So I made sure I made the most of it. Joe was telling me all along to enjoy it and experience as much as I could. So of course I went in the opening ceremony even though that meant spending hours on your feet and being exhausted afterwards. I suppose I knew if I made another Olympics it would be a lot more serious.

Sonia O'Sullivan was the only other Irish competitor in the 3,000 metres. I saw her briefly in the call room, but of course we were in separate heats. I was too innocent about the whole thing to get really nervous, and I ran as well as expected, finishing eighth in my heat in 8:57.91.

I met up with Joe a short while afterwards and we hardly even talked about the race. He just said well done, you can relax now and enjoy yourself a bit more. I suppose we really were using the whole thing as experience. I know Joe was already thinking about four years' time and the Atlanta Olympics. I knew he was going to be an awful lot more serious about it the next time.

So I went off and enjoyed myself. I actually chased down a few athletes for autographs and things like that, and of course I went to the closing ceremony as well. But even then I was looking forward to getting back into the cross-country training, and that wasn't the mindset of a true track specialist.

I think about one word when I think of the 1993 track season – blisters. It was now obvious I would be more suited to the 10,000 metres than the 3,000 metres, so that became the target for the World Championships in Stuttgart.

I qualified at the start of the summer in Hengelo by running 32:14.74, which broke the Irish record at the time. That kind of time left me in the running for a decent finish at the World Championships.

I just about got through the heats by running 33:00.38, but both my feet were badly blistered afterwards. The track in Stuttgart was a lot harder than I was used to. The final was down for two days later, and after a few laps I was in trouble. I had to drop out. I don't remember where or when, but it was the first time I'd stopped in a major race. And that annoyed me for days.

If anything, the disappointment of Stuttgart in 1993 made me more determined than ever to have a good track season the following year, and to finally answer all those people who said I wasn't reaching my full potential on the track. I decided 1994 was going to be a big year for me on the track, and I had the European Championships in Helsinki in August to aim for. What better way to prove the doubters wrong than to win the gold medal there?

So it was back to Albuquerque in May for three weeks of altitude training, which would provide the foundation for the summer. Just two weeks after I got back, Ireland's group of the Europa Cup was being held in Santry, and I agreed to run the 10,000 metres to help the team gain promotion.

I took off from the gun that day. I felt fantastic and led every step of the way, all 25 laps of the thing. There was a small-enough crowd there but I was determined to show every one of them what I could do. I crossed the finish line in 31:19.10. That knocked almost a minute off the Irish record I had run in Hengelo the year before. It was the fastest time by a European that season, and straight away people were talking about me winning the European title. I didn't see any reason why I couldn't.

For the next month or so I did some of my hardest ever training on the track. All my track sessions were done in either Lanesboro or Tullamore. Lanesboro was a cinder track, about 20 minutes or so outside Longford town. It used to take us 45 minutes or so to drive there, which seemed like a lot of hassle. And I always thought the track was just too much hassle compared to cross-country. All I had to do for cross-country training was go out the back fields or down to the golf course or wherever, and that's one of the main reasons why I enjoyed it so much. It was always on my doorstep.

And then to get to a real track we had to go to Tullamore, which was an hour and a half away. I was still working that summer so I used to meet Joe as soon as I finished, at 5.30 in the evening. We'd drive straight to Tullamore and start training at seven.

Between the warm-up and stretching and everything it would be after nine before we were finished. Then it was straight back into the car, home by 11, and straight to bed. There were some days when we'd arrive at Tullamore at seven and all I was ready for was a sleep – especially if it was a warm summer's evening.

In a way the track training became a real strain. I know I had the talent to do something really special on the track, and things would definitely have been a whole lot easier if we'd had a suitable track a little closer to home. But I would never use the lack of facilities as any sort of excuse when talking about my track career. We just made use of what we had.

There was a lot of hype about the Irish medal prospects in those European championships. Sonia was practically unbeatable on the track that summer and most people had already put the 3,000 metres gold medal around her neck. That took some of the pressure off me, but I was still fancied to get a medal of some sort in the 10,000 metres.

The team were flying out to Helsinki on the Saturday, and the Tuesday before that I went to Tullamore with Joe to do my last session. To be honest, it was probably the hardest session I ever did on the track. Not because of the quality of it, but because I had to work so hard to hit the times Joe wanted.

It was 400 fast, then 400 steady, then the same with 300 metres, 200 metres, and then 100 metres. I repeated that three times, with no one there to help me. I didn't realise it at the time but I'd pushed myself over the edge. Just a few days before that, I'd done a hard 12-kilometre run on the road, in about 39 minutes.

I remember hearing a story about a session Eamonn Coghlan did shortly before the World Championships of 1983. He was planning do to something like 20 times 400 metres.

After five or six of them he just eased up and stopped. He knew he was perfectly fit, at his absolute peak, and there was nothing left to gain from that session. He won the gold medal a week or so later, hardly breaking sweat.

The truth is I had probably gone over the edge even before that last session.

The European 10,000-metre final was set for the evening of August 13th. There were 21 runners on the start line, and I was the only one not to finish. My legs felt like strips of lead. I had no energy and felt absolutely terrible. I'd never really had a feeling like that before. I couldn't have finished that race if my life depended on it.

So just like Stuttgart a year before, I just jogged off the track and into the tunnel. All I wanted to do was sit down. After a few minutes Joe appeared.

What happened?

I don't know, I just don't know.

He couldn't speak for a while. He was just as shocked as I was.

You can be the fittest athlete on the planet, but if there's any sort of staleness in the legs then there's nothing you can do about it.

The European title was won by Portugal's Fernanda Ribeiro in a great time of 31:08.75. Second was Conceiaco Ferreira of Portugal and third was a Swiss girl, Daria Nauer, that I'd never heard much about till then.

I know I could have won a medal in that race if I'd just done things a little differently and not gone into it feeling so stale. That's the most frustrating part.

I'd say half the country was watching that race at home on RTÉ. John Treacy was coming to the end of his career and was doing some studio work for them. Somehow John had got word of the session I did on the Tuesday before. So he said it straight up that I had done this hard session and probably overtrained. All you need to do in the week before a big race like that are a few strides, he said, especially if you're feeling tired.

Of course I took it very handy for the days before the race, just a few easy runs and a few strides. But those last few sessions were just a little bit much. I should have eased back and not continued to push on. I should have allowed my body to rest and recover.

It wasn't that Joe didn't know what he was doing. The fact is so many athletes and coaches get things wrong at one time or another. Nobody gets it right all the time. I can think of a fair few who got it wrong for the cross-country.

A few days after we got back I went into Trinity for some tests. I had to get up on the treadmill and do another hard run, the last thing I wanted to do. They reckoned something was a little off balance in my blood, that I might have a minor virus or something. But I knew I was just tired. If there was a strain of virus that resulted in only one symptom then I had it: the deadly staleness virus.

The other theory was that I'd got the timing of altitude training wrong, that I'd gone too early, which can actually bring on negative effects later in the season. But I don't think that was the main reason.

Helsinki was by far the lowest point of my track career. Sonia won the 3,000 metres as expected but that made no difference to the way I felt.

Just a few days later I felt the spring coming back into my legs and ran a couple more track races to help me forget. Within a week or so it was all behind me. As long as I was able to get out running again it was like Helsinki had never happened. That proved to me that the running was far more important than the success, and not vice versa.

Two weeks after Helsinki I went to the Berlin Grand Prix to run the 5,000 metres. I'd done no hard training at all since and was feeling quite fresh again. Three laps in I hit the front, and from there until the end everyone was trying to hang on to me. As usual one or two came sprinting past, including Britain's Alison Wyeth, who was running very well at the time. But I finished third in 15:13.07, and that definitely helped get Helsinki out of my system.

I met John Treacy a few days after that, and he was very enthusiastic about my run in Berlin. He'd gone on a run with me and I think he knew I had the ability to run some great track races. He said I needed to run more 1,500-metre races, even if it meant I needed to get used to being beaten more often. But I didn't run the 1,500 metres because I just did not like being beaten, so I didn't see the point. To me it was just way, way too short.

Less than a week later the IAAF Grand Prix final was being staged at the St Denis stadium in Paris. Sonia was down to run the 5,000 metres too, but our motivation was a little different. I was just looking for another good run to help me get over Helsinki and she was looking to win the overall IAAF Grand Prix, which was worth a lot of money.

Typical of Sonia she went for it, taking off like it was a 1,500-metre race. She had about a 50-metre lead at one stage after flying through the first 1,000 metres in 2:57.3. I sat back in the pack, trying to run my own race. At 2,000 metres Sonia slowed a bit, and shortly after that I started leading the chase. I opened about five metres on everyone else and I could feel I was catching Sonia.

RTÉ would regularly show those Grand Prix meetings back then, and it must have been an amazing sight, two Irish runners leading a Grand Prix final in the 5,000 metres. Sonia was just about holding onto her lead. With three laps to go I was right on her heels, and she was visibly tiring. I ran behind her for a while, and with two laps to go I was still feeling good. Down the back straight I went up alongside her. I got about half a stride ahead, but I should have dug deeper to get past her. Straightaway Sonia seemed to recover. She had me where she wanted me, and her confidence returned.

Coming to the bell lap and she had eased back in front, and then she launched into her usual sprint. It was obvious then she was going to win. I was passed that time too by Wyeth with about 300 metres to go, and two more after that, and I ended up fifth.

I can't blame anyone but I suppose people were getting the impression that I just wasn't quite as good on the track. I heard it said afterwards that I didn't have the courage to take on Sonia. Everyone is entitled to an opinion, but Sonia ran a great race that day. She had great courage to hold onto me and come past me again.

Most people didn't realise then that I didn't like the track nearly as much as Sonia did, and I just didn't feel as comfortable running around tight bends inside those hot stadiums.

And I could write a long list of other things I didn't like about the track. It was supposed to be the glamorous side of athletics, but there was a lot of waiting around because most of the time you'd be running late in the evening, and I hated wasting time like that. And of course it would be very hot.

But I wasn't prepared to give it up just yet. The 1995 World Championships were set for Gothenburg in Sweden. It definitely wouldn't be too hot there and I'd be damn careful not to overcook the training like I did before Helsinki.

Just like the previous three years, I went into the 1995 track season with another World Cross Country silver medal around my neck. Those races at the end of 1994 proved I could run with the best of them over 5,000 metres, and if I got everything right then I knew I could run even better over 10,000 metres.

I started racing a little later than usual and opened up with a personal best of 14:59.04 when finishing second in the 5,000 metres in Paris. After that I'd planned a 10,000 metres in Lille in France on June 17th. Once again I hit the front early and reeled off lap after lap, winning in 31:08.41. That knocked 11 seconds off my own Irish record and at the time made me the sixth-fastest European ever. That did a lot for my confidence. It was my best start to a track season by a long way.

The plan this time was to go altitude training later in the summer, and Joe had picked Davos in Switzerland. We were based there from June 24th until July 18th, although I headed off to race a few times, including another 5,000 metres in Stockholm, where I ran 15:05.42

I had a few problems with my stay in Davos. We had a 15-minute bus ride every morning just to get to the lake area to go running, when all I wanted to do was head out the door and run.

I was spending lots of time on my own, so it just wasn't enjoyable. It was all becoming a little monotonous at that stage, and I definitely could have done with a bit more company. It was very hot and sticky that time of the year as well.

But the biggest problem about being in Davos was this pain in my foot. I remember first feeling it at the airport on the morning we headed out there, and deep down I knew something was wrong. The whole time I was out there the foot was causing problems, but I kept training through it, until eventually I could not run on it any more.

The last big race planned before Gothenburg was in Oslo, at the famous Bislett Games. As soon as I put my spikes on I knew I was in big trouble. I couldn't even put my foot down on the track with the pain. I cursed under my breath for a few laps and then dropped out. The pain in my foot was unbelievable.

Ger Hartmann was working out of London at that time, and Ray Flynn advised me to head over there and get some treatment.

Ger diagnosed the problem straight away as plantar fasciitis, which is essentially a badly inflamed foot muscle. The only cure is several weeks' rest. That was the end of my World Championships.

That was the first serious injury of my career, but I think I was burned out again as much as injured. If I'd had a little more cop-on I wouldn't have trained on it at all in Davos, and maybe I would have got away with it.

I went home that night almost relieved. I was wrecked. Most of the time an injury like that would be my worst nightmare. That one time though I didn't really care a whole lot. I was physically tired, and even more so mentally. The body was craving a rest.

I sat at home and watched the World Championships on television, and I was happy not to be there. The fact was I'd been five years on the go without a break. That was part of the problem. The other problem was I felt like I was only really doing the training for the track because I felt I had to, that it was my job as an athlete. Not because I wanted to. It wasn't like the cross-country, which I always wanted to run. The track was more of an assignment than anything else. And I was ready to quit.

I think I would have had a very hard time going back to the track for another year were it not for the fact that the summer of 1996 was the summer of the Atlanta Olympics. I would have been foolish not to give it one more go. I had left Barcelona in 1992 knowing I'd be back four years later. The people around me were saying it was another great chance to prove myself on the track. I knew it would be my last chance.

CHAPTER 8
BORN IN TIME

IN THE WEEKS BEFORE THE 1996 OLYMPICS IN ATLANTA YOU could ask any schoolgirl in the country who her favourite athlete was and she would tell you Sonia O'Sullivan. Ask her who her second-favourite was and she would tell you Catherina McKiernan. That suited me absolutely fine. It never bothered me for one second that Sonia was the biggest star of Irish athletics and I was the second-biggest. I don't know how I would have managed if it ever happened to be the other way around.

It is incredible to think that Sonia and myself were born within two days of each other. I know there's been something of a tradition of that in Irish sport, with Eamonn Coghlan and John Treacy coming along around the same time, and then Seán Kelly and Stephen Roche in cycling.

People automatically make comparisons in that scenario. But I never thought much about my career versus Sonia's career. The fact is our careers very rarely crossed paths.

We ran together at the World Cross Country in Boston in 1992, and after that we didn't run a championship race against each other until the World Cross Country in Turin in 1997. We met no more than two or three times in between. The main reason is we were focusing on different events over the years, because she was much more of a 1,500-metre runner early in her career.

But the other reason is that we so rarely managed to be running well at the same time. I would run well for five or six months of the year, and Sonia would run well for the other five or six months. It almost reached the stage where if Sonia was injured or sick or whatever and not running well, then it meant I had to be running well. And vice versa.

As a result of all that we never really became great rivals. The fact that we came from the same country meant some people assumed we were, but they obviously didn't realise just how rarely we actually raced together. On top of that we never really got to know each other.

I was terribly quiet around most other athletes. If people talked to me I would always talk back but I just never was one to go up to people and start conversations. And then if they started talking to me about myself I would try to bring it back to something else.

And I was quiet towards Sonia, no doubt about it. I just felt that anything I said would come across as intrusive. Such as where are you running next? Or how's the training going? I was sure she was sick of people asking her that. I knew what it was like to be asked those questions and they usually drove me mad. And so what else was I going to ask her?

And we definitely never hung out together. I was mainly based in Ireland and Sonia wasn't. Of course I would see her now and again in passing but never said much more than hello. We were both focused on different things really, getting ready for our own targets. Obviously if we'd been running the same races more often we could have become quite serious rivals.

We'd sometimes share a bus journey before or after a race, and all we'd say is well done, and that was about it. That was just the way it worked.

The first time I got to spend even a small amount of time with Sonia was at the 1992 Olympics in Barcelona. I remember saying hello once or twice, and I have this photograph somewhere of a group of us, and I'm standing with Sonia. That was as close as we got to each other the whole time we were there.

Most athletes do their own thing at the Olympics. A lot of us went down to the boxing arena the day Michael Carruth won his gold medal, but I didn't hang around for the celebrations. As usual I went straight back to bed. Later that night the whole Irish crew came back to the village and were shouting and roaring at some unearthly hour. They took the place over, and I remember thinking the rest of the teams in the village must have thought we were all mad.

Even after the 1994 Grand Prix final, when I very nearly beat Sonia, we didn't say much. Afterwards people made it sound like that was the height of our rivalry. I probably should have beaten her that day, but I just didn't have the confidence to do that on the track. Like I can't pass her, not on the track. This was her stage. One of my brothers really gave me a hard time about that. What were you thinking? Why didn't you just go by her?

What very few people realised was that I was glad Sonia was so successful at the same time, that I was delighted she was around when I was. If she hadn't been around I reckon my career would have been a lot shorter.

For a start I wasn't a big fan of all the awards ceremonies. I just loved to run and run hard. I never wanted to be asked to a function. I appreciated all the offers I got. But there were times I wished it would all go away. It comes with the territory, Peadar would say.

For instance, I have been invited to the Áras for different events and feel very privileged to be asked. Last time I was there I got to the table before Martin and President Mary McAleese arrived in. When I saw the big dining table and my place name next to the President and her husband, I just had to do a quick switch and put Damien sitting beside them. I was just too shy. I could chat casually with them – but for two or three hours what could I talk about? At least Damien is able to talk to anyone. But Martin McAleese is a big athletics fan and I got to know him running in the Phoenix Park. Both he and President McAleese are very friendly and down to earth, and what's more, I would run by their house every day.

Going into the 1996 Olympics in Atlanta both Sonia and myself were at something of a peak in our careers. I had won four silver medals in the World Cross Country and gold in the European cross-country and still had the potential to be one of the best 10,000-metre runners around. Sonia had won the European Championship 3,000 metres and the World Championship 5,000 metres and by then was the best 5,000-metre runner around.

If Sonia had not been there at the same time then I would have been carrying all the hopes into those Olympics Games. And I would not have liked that. All that was expected of me was to go out there and run my best, and if everything went to plan I might just sneak a medal. Sonia was expected to go there and win.

Despite the disappointments of the previous three track seasons, I was still determined to prepare in the best way possible for Atlanta. So as usual Joe and I planned out a series of races that we felt would get me to peak on August 2nd, the night of the Olympic 10,000-metre final.

I started off the season with a trip to Osaka in Japan for an early 5,000 metres. Now that was a long way to go for a track race. Of course there was good money for it, and they were willing to pay a good appearance fee for the four-time World Cross Country silver medallist.

By then Longford agent Ray Flynn had taken over as my agent, and he always did a great job in getting me the races where and when I wanted. He set up his business in Tennessee shortly after he retired from his own brilliant track career – he still holds the Irish 1,500-metre and mile records. Once I started working with Ray I never had any reason to look for another agent. He is a great guy, and as far as I'm concerned the best man in the world to represent athletes.

The amazing thing about those trips to places like Osaka is that I could have been anywhere. I certainly wasn't rushing out to buy the *Rough Guide* to Osaka before I left. I would arrive in after this cruelly long flight and then find I wasn't able to sleep that night. I always found that terrible. As soon as I arrived in Japan I couldn't wait to get back home. Joe wouldn't come because there was no point, so I'd be there entirely on my own. So those trips to Japan were spent almost entirely sleeping and trying to recover from the flight.

Anyway, I won there in 15:07.31, not bad at all for an opening track race. About a week later I ran what was then a personal best of 14:58.65 in Hengelo, finishing third behind the Ethiopians Derartu Tulu and Gete Wami. That was a very good run, but then I was still fresh. Still, I reckon those hard, fast races did take a lot out of me. They would grind me down.

My sister Rose got married on June 2nd, and I was bridesmaid. I left the wedding reception early, because I was going to Paris the next day for another 5,000-metre race. It was well worth the trip though as I was second in another personal best, 14:55.39. Tulu sat behind me most of the way and of course beat me in the sprint.

I did wonder a small bit if I was running a little too well too soon. On the

Coming home to win the
2004 Flora Women's Dublin
mini-marathon

Clockwise from top left: With Fr McNamara on my confirmation day in Killeshandra, May 1983

All smiles after a race win in the early 1990s

Wearing my best poncho at the Confirmation of Peadar and Seán in 1973. Eileen, Dympna, and Rose lend support as my mother keeps count. My father and Thomas are at home working on the farm

Snapped in a photo booth on a trip to Salthill in 1984

Posing in the front garden of our house in 1975

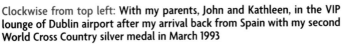

Clockwise from top left: **With my parents, John and Kathleen, in the VIP lounge of Dublin airport after my arrival back from Spain with my second World Cross Country silver medal in March 1993**

Damien and myself on our wedding day in Coronea Church, Cornafean, November 25th, 2000

Making my big arrival at Coronea Church

John Treacy presents me with a piece of cut crystal to mark my silver-medal run in Spain. The photograph was taken in the Council Chamber of Cavan Courthouse, where I was working at the time

My friend Deirdre Martin lends moral support at an awards dinner in the early 1990s

Deirbhile entertains Damien and me at home in Castleknock, summer 2005

Clockwise from top left: I congratulate Sonia O'Sullivan, and she returns the compliment, after she finished ahead of me in the 2003 Women's Mini Marathon in Dublin

My friend and rival Paula Radcliffe shows typically battling form at a race in Portugal in 2000

Leaning into a corner at the 1995 World Cross Country in Durham, where I beat everyone except Derartu Tulu

The former Taoiseach Albert Reynolds congratulates me after my win at Rás na hÉireann, on Dundalk racecourse, February 2004

The legendary Haile Gebrselassie and myself hang onto the adidas Dublin Marathon race director, Jim Aughney, a legend in his own right, during a publicity run in London, 2005

Struggling to stay with the pace during the 2003 European Cross Country in Edinburgh, a race that brought team silver for Ireland but left me in tears after my 34th-place finish

Crossing Tower Bridge, second from right and full of confidence, after 20 kilometres of the 1998 London Marathon. Liz McColgan (who finished second) is second from left

Clockwise from top left: The ever-watchful Joe Doonan, my coach through all my most successful years, keeps tabs on race splits during the 1998 Amsterdam marathon

Flying the flag, and the tinfoil, after my London marathon win in 1998

Crossing the line in London 1998 in a time of 2:26:26, probably my greatest, and certainly my most famous, win

Still keen to win, even in my farewell run, I stretch away from the field in the Annalee, Cavan, 10-kilometre road race, October 2004

Harry Gorman, one of the great athletics supporters, congratulates me after the 1998 Amsterdam marathon

Just off the pace before going on to win at Rás na hÉireann, Dundalk racecourse, February 2004

Running at full tilt in the 10,000 metre final at the 1993 World Championships in Stuttgart. Blisters forced me out of the race.

track it's a fine line between sharpening your fitness and running yourself down, and you can overdo it quite easily. Having Joe watching me at training all the time meant I was trying to get the times he talked about. Not to impress him or anything. It just felt like I needed to do the sessions he wanted if I was going to run the times I wanted. If I had been left on my own a little more I probably would have run more like I felt. Or not gone to certain races when I just felt like training. It was also very hard work doing all those track sessions alone, and I'd sometimes be a lot more nervous about getting through the sessions than the races. If I'd had someone there to help drag me around maybe then they wouldn't have been so draining.

To confirm your place on the Irish team in Atlanta you had to run in the National Championships in Santry, and I won the 5,000 metres without much hassle in 15:27.10. At that stage the build-up to Atlanta was going exactly to plan, and the hype about the Olympics was building up too.

Straight after the Nationals I headed off to altitude training, this time to Font Romeau in France. Joe had agreed to do some coaching for Noel Berkeley and he came along too, even though he had just missed out on the Olympics.

The very first day we got there we met Paula Radcliffe, who by then was using the place a lot. So we agreed to meet for a run the following morning. She led the way up this trail, and it was unbelievably rocky, with roots sticking up everywhere. It was hard to run on and I was sure I was going to break my ankle. Paula was obviously used to it. But we didn't run on that trail again. In fact I did almost all my running around football pitches. Besides, Joe believed it was an advantage to train alone if you wanted to be a truly world-class runner. Looking back, I always preferred to have company while running and training.

At least Noel helped make that trip a little more enjoyable, and Font Romeau is a nice plan to train.

Paula bought an apartment in Font Romeau and that is her home away from home. She invited me up to dinner and I did get to know her well. But of course I didn't see her as a rival at all. She was studying a lot and seemed to be injured a lot while I was running cross-country, and she'd only ever beaten me once – in Mallusk a couple of years earlier.

I never realised she would make such a major breakthrough, but she has the dedication, and her main strength is her mental and physical toughness. She obviously has a very high pain threshold.

After Font Romeau I was home for three days and then headed straight out to Atlanta. Nearly all the talk in the build-up to those Olympics was about the heat and humidity, and how it was going to kill us all. Joe figured the sooner I started acclimatising the better. Ray Flynn had arranged for me to stay with an Irishman called Mike Fitzgerald, just outside Atlanta.

The flight over wasn't so bad, but when we got inside the airport there was a long queue of athletes and coaches waiting to get their accreditation. Joe took one look at it. Right, he said, we're skipping this. Next thing I know we're at the front of the queue being handed our accreditations. That was typical of Joe. He wasn't going to let bad organisation get in his way.

That was the easy part. Then we walked outside, and for the first time I got the full blast of the Atlanta heat. It was unbelievable, nothing like I'd ever experienced before. I just looked at Joe. He said nothing.

God help me. How am I going to run six miles in this?

Joe's plan was to get used to it day by day. So that meant getting up at six the following morning for my first run. He thought it couldn't be so bad at that hour. So I set the alarm and was delighted to wake up to some nice, cool air. I didn't realise that was just the air conditioning. Once I opened the front door the heat hit me full blast. I'd planned on running with a T-shirt over my vest, but I swapped those straight away for a belly-top. I was sweating quite badly on that run, but the fact is you did get used to it. I suppose the heat was just playing on my mind. I felt I wasn't prepared for this.

We stayed at that Fitzgerald's house for about eight days. Mike and his wife were very nice, but as always I was getting a little homesick, so on one of the days I took a loan of a bicycle. Of course I fell off and managed to bash my knee against the road. I knew it wasn't anything serious but I still didn't want to tell Joe about it. I went back to the house and washed and thought I could cover it up for the following day's run. But of course I had to wear shorts because of the heat or else Joe would know something was wrong. Another reason to curse the heat. So Joe got an awful fright when he saw the knee. I knew it was just a cut but he was panicking, thinking it might be something worse.

After a week there I went to the athletes' village, and it was great to meet the other athletes. Except that the accommodation in the village was terrible – tiny little beds and cement floors. But that wasn't going to take from my performance and I wasn't complaining.

The worst part was that you had to share the shower with four other people, so every time you went in there, the place was drenched. The rest of the village was okay, but the accommodation was really quite rough. That certainly wasn't part of the Olympic dream that athletes think about.

I was sharing a room with Marie McMahon, the young Clare runner who had qualified for the 5,000 metres. She ended up having a real nightmare when the medicine she was taking for a slight head cold showed up as a positive doping sample. When she got back that night her eyes were swollen and bloodshot from all the crying, and I felt very sorry for her. She had made a genuine mistake. If something like that had ever happened to me I don't know how I would have coped.

My heat was scheduled for Saturday, July 27th – and the worst part about it was the time, something like 10.30 at night. I managed to finish sixth in 32:32.10, easily qualifying for the final, with Gete Wami winning and the big Chinese threat, Wang Junxia, just behind me in seventh.

Derartu Tulu won the second heat. Everybody was going to be there and everybody was running well. But I felt quite good the whole way and had no trouble staying with the pace. They had sponges laid out on the back straight. They were soaked in cold water and I used them quite a bit to stay cool.

When I met Joe in the tunnel afterwards he looked quite relieved. For the first time it looked like I had peaked for a major championship on the track. Joe said something about using the sponges too much, but he wasn't the one out there on the track suffering from the heat.

I did a one-hour run the next day and everything felt fine. There were five days before the final the following Friday, so you had to do something to stay sharp, and on one of those days I did four times 1,000 metres. I was definitely not going to overdo things.

The week wasn't long passing. Like everyone else I sat down on the Sunday night to watch Sonia in the final of the 5,000 metres, having no idea what was about to happen.

It's hard for me to even imagine what Sonia must have gone through, and the infamous tunnel incident – where she was ordered to change her vest before going onto the track for her race – was something I never really got to hear about in any great detail. Even from the television pictures it was very clear she was struggling from early in the race. She was just covered in sweat, and every athlete knows that's not a good thing. It was difficult to watch, but I wasn't shocked when she dropped out. I just knew she wasn't right, that she wasn't going to win no matter how hard she tried. Something was obviously badly wrong with her. I felt terribly sorry for her and what she was going through.

I never even saw Sonia at any stage afterwards, or for a long time after that. Obviously she was under incredible pressure coming into those Olympics. The truth is I never had to deal with pressure quite like that. And in a strange way part of that was all because of Sonia. She was expected to do well on the track and I was expected to do well in cross-country. I know if she wasn't running those track championships at the same time then the spotlight would have been turned on me. And that would have brought pressure for sure.

So sitting in the tunnel before my Olympic final I wasn't so much nervous as anxious. I'd had problems before with blisters, especially on the track, and even more so when it was hot. So I was just hoping the shoes would be okay and the feet wouldn't cause any problems. And by then we'd heard stories about the track in Atlanta, that it was particularly hard for the distance runners. It's fine for the sprinters, but Haile Gebrselassie had his feet cut badly in winning the 10,000 metres and couldn't run the 5,000 metres as a result.

There was only one way I was going to run that race and that was from the front. The strategy was simple: try to burn off as many runners as I could and then hold my position as long as I could. If that went exactly to plan then anything was possible.

It was a strange kind of race, because I did feel quite good out there. I got to the front as planned and led through the first 3,000 metres in 9:17. But most of the field was just lined up behind me. I don't know how much the heat had to do with it but when the pace gradually picked up after halfway I just wasn't able to go with the leaders. I knew then I wasn't going to win an Olympic medal, but I kept pressing on. In the back of my mind I probably realised this was going to be one of my last major races on the track, and I might as well give it my all. In the end I crossed the line in 11th place, in 32:00.38. Fernanda Ribeiro of Portugal had run an amazing race to beat Wang, with Wami and Tulu third and fourth.

Olympic final, 11th place: they were the only words I wrote in my diary that night. I still think it was good running in those conditions. At least I survived it without getting any blisters. And it was a satisfying run. I think Joe was happy enough, but I remember my brother Peadar saying afterwards that I might have been using the heat as a bit of an excuse.

Maybe if I'd made the top 10 I'd have been a little more satisfied, but it certainly wasn't a bad run. And I wasn't dying for a break afterwards. I was glad I'd come through a major championship without feeling I needed a holiday. All things considered, I believe I ran as well as I could.

The fact is I was the best Irish finisher on the track at those Olympics. I still look back on Atlanta with a satisfied mind. I'd proven to myself that I could at least perform well at a major track championship. I'd run 50 laps of that track in Atlanta and my legs were still in reasonable shape, and I was actually excited at the prospect of running a few more races afterwards.

There was a small welcome-home party at Dublin airport. Some of my nephews were at the age where they realised the Olympics were a big event, and they were obviously delighted to see me. In a way I was glad to have got through it. I still think I would have run a little better if it hadn't been so hot. I know it's the same for everyone, but some athletes are more used to it. Not just the Africans, but the Spanish and the Portuguese as well.

One of the first Grand Prix meetings after Atlanta was in Cologne in Germany, and most of the big names were running the 5,000 metres. It turned out to be one of the fastest races of the year, and I managed to knock nearly 10 seconds off my personal best when finishing seventh in 14:49.40. That was one of the fastest times ever by a European and just eight seconds off Sonia's Irish record set the previous summer. That was definitely one of the most satisfying runs on the track.

After that I went to the Grand Prix final in Brussels and finished sixth in 15:07.34, just a stride behind Paula Radcliffe. We were more or less running at the same level then, even on the track. Paula had finished fifth in the Olympic 5,000 metres but a bit like myself just didn't quite have the finishing speed to compete for the medals.

That was the end of another track season. I never got the same feeling of satisfaction at the end of a track season as I did after a cross-country season, but I felt reasonably satisfied after that summer. I'd run some very good times and performed as well as I could have at the Olympic Games. Overall then it was my best season on the track. I just didn't quite realise at the time that it was also my last one. I had in fact run my last races on the track.

There are people who believe the track is the truest test of running ability. It is a lot more high-profile, but I wouldn't necessarily agree. I don't think that just because I never really made it to the very top of the track I'm any less of an athlete than those who did.

It's possible that I didn't always do the best kind of training. I know when I started doing the really fast stuff on the track I started losing my edge. I was definitely getting tired a little quicker than I normally would and finding it harder to recover. But a lot of that had to do with the tiredness that had built up over the cross-country season.

Success on the track also meant a far higher profile, and I certainly never chased that. I was more than satisfied with the profile I had. Most of the time I would go into the shops and just hope no one would recognise me. I can hardly remember a time when I didn't have that pressure constantly bearing down on my back. It must have been when I was 16 or 17. When you're born with as much shyness as I was it takes a long time to lose it

I'd also go to Mass on a Sunday and have to make a quick exit or else people would be asking me questions about my running. I didn't mind them asking my parents or any of the brother or sisters. Like saying to them they saw me on the television and I was looking very well. I didn't mind that at all. I'd be happy to see them asked. Just don't ask me. It was only as the years went on that I got used to it and was able to deal with it all with far more confidence.

Some people might say I didn't have the killer instinct to be truly successful on the track. I wouldn't necessarily agree with that either. I never lacked that killer instinct when it came to cross-country. When I won the European cross-country in 1994 I had to call on all the killer instinct I had. First of all we were nearly led astray early in that race, I had to cut under the barriers to make sure I stayed on course. There was an awful wind to contend with that day too. And just when I thought I had it won, Julia Vaquero came up alongside me, and I just stuck my elbows out, as if to say get away from me. I wasn't going to lose that one. She was breathing right down my back, but I had to win that one. I don't think I could have handled finishing second there. By then I knew I was the best cross-country runner in Europe and I proved I had the killer instinct to ensure I won.

It would have been nice if I'd won that title a few more times. In 1995 I had a slight problem with cartilage in my knee and needed a small operation in England that December. And in December of 1996 I was only half training with an Achilles injury.

But I have no real regrets about my cross-country career and no real regrets about my track career either. My 31:08.41 for 10,000 metres is still the 16th-fastest time ever run by a European-born woman. It stood as the Irish record for five years.

I took a short break after Atlanta, but soon got back into my usual routine, preparing for another cross-country season. The plan was to build towards the 1997 World Cross Country as usual, but for the first time in my career the marathon wasn't just on the horizon – it was coming into view.

I turned 27 in November of 1996, and that was definitely the right age to start thinking about the marathon. Those championships in Turin in 1997 marked my ninth consecutive appearance in the World Cross Country since I'd made my debut in Stavanger in 1989. I think everyone around me agreed it was time for a change.

CHAPTER 9
TIMES CHANGE

IT WAS PROBABLY INEVITABLE THAT I WOULD MEET MY FUTURE husband through running. A lot of athletes meet their husbands or wives on the athletics circuit, and there are quite a few who have married either their coach or another athlete.

But Damien O'Reilly wasn't a runner. He was and still is a journalist. Of all the professions in the world, I find someone who's a journalist! After all the years I spent trying to avoid them, or more specifically, their questions. Well, opposites obviously attract.

Our first face-to-face meeting didn't happen in Ireland. There was no romantic setting either. It was March of 1995, when I was competing at the World Cross Country championships in Durham in the north of England.

Damien came over to cover the event for the local radio station in Cavan, Shannonside Northern Sound. They didn't normally send reporters outside of Cavan to cover anything, least of all a cross-country race. Damien had obviously helped convince them that I was worth reporting on, since most people in Cavan had begun to take a huge interest in my career.

And they weren't all athletics enthusiasts. I began to discover that people from all walks of life and many from a predominantly GAA background were now following my career closely, proud that I was flying the Cavan flag.

That day in Durham I won my fourth successive silver medal in the World Cross Country. The specialist athletics journalists figured that must have been a disappointment, to finish second yet again. But when Damien interviewed me for his radio station he was a little more excited and figured another silver medal was fantastic. That was the way I saw it too, and I suppose I liked him for that. In fact at the post-race press conference, I gave him the first interview. And as all the other journalists crowded round to take quotes from this first exclusive interview he was under pressure to ask the right questions.

His father Paddy also travelled over. He is from Cavan and was delighted on two fronts: to see me winning and his son getting this "important" interview with me. Like most Cavan people he had kept tabs on my career since my run in the 1992 Boston marathon although I don't think he ever imagined his son would end up marrying me.

I finished off by thanking Damien, Shannonside/Northern Sound and all my supporters back in Cavan. Damien was delighted with this scoop, and it made him quite popular with his bosses back in the station, who had tried and failed so often to get a decent interview with me.

He called me up once or twice over the next year requesting an interview for the radio. And I was glad to oblige. A lot of people listened to that station, and Damien would never ask me any hard questions. Just the way I liked it.

Although Damien was raised in Dublin he'd told me all about his Cavan background and I liked that about him too. His father, Paddy, was from Bally-jamesduff. Like a lot of Cavan people of his generation, Paddy moved in the 1960s to Dublin, where he became a successful publican. He met Pauline, an Offaly woman, and they got married and had four children, Damien being the eldest, and lived in Castleknock.

When he was a child Damien spent many holidays on the farm in Bally-jamesduff with his grandmother, Margaret O'Reilly and uncle Philip. He became very familiar with Cavan and with country life, so when we met we had more in common than I ever thought would be possible between me and a Dublin-born journalist.

Following that initial meeting in Durham, we spoke only by phone in radio interviews. There was nothing else to it at that stage, though he had managed to get me to talk more freely in interviews than I had ever done before.

The next time we met was a year later, again at the World Cross Country, this time in Cape Town, South Africa. There was some dispute going on at the time within European broadcasting and Damien ended up covering the event for several radio stations at home. He was the only Irish journalist who made it out there.

Damien was keen to take full advantage of the situation and figured there had to be a few more important people he could interview out there as well as Catherina McKiernan. When we did get to meet after my race he told me he'd also interviewed Nelson Mandela earlier in the day. It was probably more like a quote, but apparently he'd spotted the South African president mingling with crowds close to the finish line.

What happened was that after finishing his sound check he mentioned to his station manager, Joe Finnegan, that he had just spotted Mandela. Get down there quick, said Joe. Try to get a few words, and you can name your price when you get home. Luckily for Damien he had height on his side – he's six foot three, exactly the same height as Mandela. He got his interview but he never told me how much it was worth. He still has the piece on tape somewhere.

We had made an initial little connection but it was more than a year later before anything really came of it. I was still completely consumed by running.

We met yet again at the World Cross Country in Turin in 1997, when Damien somehow managed to bluff his way onto one of the buses taking runners to the celebration dinner. He was on his third assignment to the World Cross Country championships, specifically to report on me.

That night was probably the first time we talked about things other than running and without a microphone getting in the way. We got on very well and I left Turin thinking he was definitely becoming a good friend.

By the end of May 1997 I'd decided it was time to move out of the family home in Cornafean. I was 27 years old. I wasn't rushed out and certainly wasn't forced out. I just felt like having a bit more breathing space. Two years previously I'd invested some of my winnings in property in Dublin, with the intention of maybe moving there some day.

Peadar was among those who advised me to invest in property at the time, and needless to say, it was good advice. And, in the case of Dublin, it truly was a matter of location, location, location. My house had to be within reach of a good place to run, and as far as I was concerned the Phoenix Park was the best place in the world to run. If anyone asked me to design the perfect training ground for distance runners I would show them the Phoenix Park. That's why I bought a house right beside one of the gates into the Park.

Straight away I knew it was one of the best moves of my life. It was around that time that I could train as long and as hard as I wanted.

One evening I was in the nearby Blanchardstown shopping centre when Gerry Carr and his wife, Jean, both serious runners, recognised me and we got chatting. Gerry was involved with the Civil Service club and had lots of running friends. He offered to meet me any evening and show me some of the trails in the Phoenix Park, and so within a few weeks I was sharing some of my long runs with Gerry and up to a dozen of his friends. They were all brilliantly welcoming and friendly, and better still, great company on the long runs.

As the summer spread into June and July I was finding my life tasted sweeter almost by the day, just having this wider circle of friends and greater variety to my life. Joe and I had finally made the decision that this was the year to move up to the marathon and leave the shorter races on the track and cross-country behind me, temporarily at least.

I'd agreed to run the Berlin marathon in September, which offered a fast course but didn't attract the truly elite fields of some bigger city marathons. I was surprised at how easy I found the marathon training compared to some of the more intense training I would have done for track and cross-country. The marathon training was less about quality and more about quantity. Being in such a pleasant environment helped make that training all the more enjoyable.

The other rooms in the house in Castleknock were rented to Linda Maxwell from Longford and Emer Smith from Cavan. And in the house next door were five other girls, all from Mayo: Celine, Niamh, Cora, Gráinne and Teresa. Cora and Gráinne were sisters and they were all great fun. We were all in our mid-20s, in the prime of our lives. It was only then that I really got to see a whole other side to life.

They were all going out at the weekends, planning trips away, all that kind of stuff. There was always a bit of atmosphere around, and I really enjoyed that. It was a side of life I'd never got to taste before.

All those things – moving to Dublin, meeting Gerry and his friends, the girls next door, the bit of fun – helped give my running a new lease of life. I didn't quite realise it at the time but that was exactly what I needed, because both physically and mentally I'd come close to being worn out by my old routine.

The best thing about those girls was that they never talked about running, asking about this race or that race. They were more interested in having parties. Any excuse would do. It felt like I was just one of them, even though I was still in bed at 10 o'clock most nights. Yet I still didn't have even the slightest temptation to join them in the pub any of the nights. And it wasn't just because of the running. I was just never into that, never a drinker. I was lucky in a way that I didn't want to do it and didn't need to do it. I didn't ever miss it and never will.

In early June I got an invitation to Deirdre Martin's wedding in Cavan. Deirdre was one of the four students in my class when I started primary school in Coronea, and she remained a good friend all during our school years. I got to see less and less of her as running gradually took over my life, but when her wedding invitation arrived I realised straight away that this was one event I wasn't going to miss.

I think if that wedding had been a year or two earlier I wouldn't have gone. I would have found a way out of it. But by moving to Dublin I'd discovered at least some daylight outside of my running and for a change something inside of me wanted to go.

She was delighted when I phoned to say I was coming. She wouldn't have taken no for an answer anyway.

And who are you going to bring? It was the question I had expected and I knew what was coming next.

Sure no one, I said. I'm coming on my own.

Forget about it. There's no way you're coming on your own. You're not coming at all unless you bring someone.

And that really was the start of it all. I called up Damien and asked him if he'd come to the wedding. He kindly obliged. It wasn't the easiest conversation in my life but it had nothing to do with the pressure.

We agreed to meet later in the week, just for a chat. Damien was still working in Cavan, and I was settled in Castleknock. We started meeting most weekends. Within a few weeks we were going out to share a meal, and then maybe to the pub for a drink. Or we'd go to the cinema the odd time.

It wasn't like my life changed overnight. That I was hanging around in night-clubs on a Friday. Damien wasn't into that scene either, so it wasn't like I was holding him back.

And I never thought for a second that Damien was going to interfere with my running or be a threat to my dedication. I know some people did think he would be a hindrance to my career. But from the very beginning he was totally considerate of my running – he didn't interfere in any way.

If anything, I found myself enjoying the running even more. I was going out a little bit more, and enjoying it too. I felt like this lifestyle was slowly creeping up on me – that this was a lifestyle I wanted a lot more now, rather than the strict regime I had lived by for so long. It was a good mix.

I wanted a change. It wasn't always deliberate, and it was probably even more gradual than it should have been, but I've no doubt now that Damien came along at just the right time. It was just starting to dawn on me that time was moving on, and I was definitely ready to see another side of life. Or more like get on with my life.

Living in Dublin helped in that other things in my life were changing, and people had to realise that.

It took a while though for Damien to get a grip on exactly what he was dealing with. He enjoyed a pint but I didn't drink at all. He wasn't a night bird but I'd be in bed at 10. And I know he thought what I was eating was a little different. I liked my food plain and simple and would happily eat my pasta without any sauce and my potatoes without any butter. He believed in a little more variety, or at least something more imaginative.

My target for that autumn of 1997, the Berlin marathon, was approaching. Damien was thinking about coming over to the race and I definitely wanted him there. Of course Joe and Peadar had planned everything about that race weeks in advance – when we'd leave, where I'd stay, and so on.

The race was on Sunday, September 28th. We'd been seeing each other a couple of months by then but the day before we were all due to leave, Peadar rang Damien at work and more or less laid down the law, but in a friendly way.

Don't be asking her any obvious questions, he said, like did she sleep well – in case she didn't sleep well. And on the morning of the race try to give her time and space.

So of course I didn't even see Damien on the morning of the race. The day before the race he went off around the city on his own. But he didn't mind. Damien was into his sport, but this whole scene was totally new to him, so he was glad to blend into the background.

By now I was totally familiar with the life of an elite runner. Picked up at the airport, brought to a five-star hotel, and generally treated like royalty. But this kind of treatment was all new to Damien. My clothing sponsors, adidas, were also sponsoring the race and gave him some athletics gear, and that pleased him no end. He was getting a feel for what it was like to be involved in elite sport, and being a sports fanatic he was lapping it up.

I firmly believe Damien prolonged my career. Suddenly I was able to give someone else satisfaction, allow him share the experience of it all. That shouldn't have been the main reason why I was still running at the highest level but the truth is it was.

The race started under the old Brandenburg Gate, in the heart of Berlin. It was a beautiful September morning, not too warm, and the air gently cleansed by a calm breeze. Damien had arranged to meet up with Frank Greally and Seán Callan. Frank is the editor of *Irish Runner* magazine and Seán is one of a famous trio of running supporters – the other two being Harry Gorman and Matt Rudden – who have travelled the world since the 1960s for almost every major race and every major championship.

Frank came over to wish me well, just as I was tying my shoelaces. But Damien was too apprehensive to come near me so close to the start. He was certain that if anything at all went wrong over the next 26.2 miles of running he'd get the blame for messing up my routine. I know he was as relieved as I was when the race worked out exactly as planned. I won the race without any problems, and we could finally enjoy each other's company for the rest of the day.

It was the following May before Damien moved back to Dublin, at first back to his old family home in Castleknock. That was when he started working full-time as a reporter for RTÉ radio. We saw a lot of each other during the summer of 1998, including a few days together in Kerry, a place we both love to visit, after I'd run the London marathon. By then I suppose we were both thinking about marriage, and when he proposed to me in December of 1998, I didn't have to think twice about saying yes.

I could never have imagined that two years later, on my wedding day, November 25th, 2000, running would be so far from my mind. For the first time in my life I realised I was looking at my life beyond running, at the prospect of married life, of settling down together and starting a family.

We were married at the Church of the Immaculate Conception in Coronea, just outside of Arva. Afterwards we all headed to the Slieve Russell Hotel in Ballyconnell, right next to where I'd done so many of my hard training runs over the years.

After the meal I stood up to say a few words of thanks and finished off by saying I would like to get back running and maybe win another big marathon. Everyone in the room stood up and gave me a big clap, but deep down I had real doubts. I doubted if I'd still have the hunger and I doubted if I still had the ability. It wasn't going to be easy.

After the usual Christmas and New Year distractions it was time to get back to the old routine if I was serious about getting back to competitive running. I had suspected it was going to be difficult and I was right. It was quite obvious I just didn't have the same level of hunger, that my desire to go and train hard every day wasn't coming back as quickly as I thought it would.

The World Cross Country championships of 2001 had been awarded to Ireland and were set for Leopardstown racecourse in Dublin at the end of March. Sonia O'Sullivan was committed to running, and the pressure was on me to join her. If we both ran anywhere close to our best then there was a strong chance we could help win team medals for Ireland.

That was exactly the kind of pressure I didn't want. It took nothing at all for me to pull out of that race. I just told the Irish athletics federation at the start of the year there was no way I'd be fit to run a World Cross Country, and I don't think they were too surprised to hear it. As it turned out, the foot-and-mouth outbreak meant they had to move the championships to Ostend in Belgium, with just two weeks' notice.

By April I'd managed to get myself back into reasonable shape. In terms of fitness I was still miles away from where I needed to be to run another marathon, but the plan was to try a few low-key races just to test the engine.

On Easter Sunday there was a four-mile road race in Dunboyne, just a few miles up the road from Castleknock. I jumped in there unannounced and managed to win it.

For the next few days I couldn't help feeling my heart wasn't in this any more, that I wasn't enjoying the training and I was dreading the thought of racing. Suddenly I didn't have to worry about that any more. At the end of August 2001, at the launch of the adidas Dublin Marathon, I announced I was pregnant. That put an end to all the speculation that I was ready to have another crack at the marathon in the autumn or the following spring.

Deirbhile was born the following March 7th, 2002. I was now a married mother and felt as far removed from running as I'd ever felt in my life.

For three or four months after Deirbhile was born I had very little interest in getting involved again with competitive running. Some days I just wished people would say to me well done, you've had a great career, and now get on with the rest of your life. I would have been happy to hang up the runners and do just that. Instead the only thing people asked was when I would get back running.

The fact was running had drifted farther from my mind than ever before. Mentally I just wasn't able to work my way back into it, and physically I was tired and drained. I was 32 years old and realising that no matter what kind of training I did now my best years were probably behind me.

But one of the things people were telling me was that I would come back even stronger after the birth of Deirbhile. It's been proven that women can get physically stronger after giving birth, particularly in terms of distance running.

The World Cross Country took place on Leopardstown racecourse in March 2002. I was invited to Leopardstown as a guest, and Damien and myself brought along Deirbhile, who was just three weeks old. I talked briefly with Sonia that day, mostly about the joys of motherhood. But I can't say I wasn't impressed by the way she had got back running so quickly, and how she was still able to compete at the highest level. And this was after the birth of her second daughter.

Something else talked about around that time was how all her old hunger for running had come back after childbirth. That was a fresh source of motivation; it told me that maybe the well wasn't yet dry. Something was still burning inside of me, a flame of hope that I could make it back to the top if I really put my mind to it. Although I was 32 there were plenty of runners around at that age who were still winning major championship races.

What I didn't feel like doing was forcing myself back into the long, hard slog of marathon training. That had taken so much out of me. And as always I wasn't just thinking about myself, but that I should be running for the family and friends and neighbours who had always supported me. Though at this stage they would probably be as happy if I just concentrated on family life, which was proving far more enjoyable now anyway.

I did want to get back running just to enjoy the feeling of being fit. But despite what people were saying about coming back even stronger after childbirth I did wonder if I'd ever be able to run a fast marathon again. I knew myself what it took to produce 26.2 miles of hard running on the roads. I'd been there, and done that. I just wasn't sure if I'd be able to do it again.

CHAPTER 10
MARATHON WOMAN

IF THERE IS SUCH A THING AS A HUMAN ENGINE DESIGNED specifically to run a marathon then I was probably born with it. When I first did the physiological testing in the human-performance laboratories of Trinity College back in 1990 all the results suggested I would run a fast marathon someday. My lung capacity, the efficiency with which I used up oxygen when running, and even my body weight and make-up were ideally suited to running long distances. It was almost like a simple scientific experiment: do the necessary training and the result would be a fast marathon.

Except that if it were that straightforward then there would be a lot more people in the world running fast marathon times. Instead there are only a select few. That's because there are still a lot more things you have to get right to run 26.2 miles at between five and six minutes per mile. There's the right pace and even the tactics, there's the fuel and water to take in along the way, and depending on how you feel, there might be a certain barrier known as the wall to break through.

There have been plenty of long-distance runners like me down through the years that assumed they could make the jump up to the marathon without any problems. Some of them made it quite successfully but I'd say there's been a lot more that haven't. I know it's been said that the marathon is a sort of graveyard of distance runners. Athletes have moved up to the marathon and it hasn't suited them.

It was with all that in mind that Joe and I sat down after the 1997 World Cross Country in Turin. My seventh-place finish was very satisfying considering the Achilles tendon that had hampered my training at the start of the season. I think deep down we both knew that if I did decide to commit 100 per cent to the marathon then it probably meant the end of my cross-country career, at least temporarily. And we both knew that also meant I would probably never win a world cross-country title.

I was happy to go along with the plan of running a marathon. As they say, a change is as good as a rest. What was certain was that I didn't want to do another track season. I had run some good times in 1996 but I couldn't face going back to that lonesome training on the track. I was totally fed up with it. In the end it just seemed everything was pointing towards the marathon, that the time was now ripe to go picking. Joe phoned Ray Flynn and asked him to line up a marathon for the autumn. There was no turning back now.

Within a few weeks we'd agreed on Berlin, set for September 28th. It was a good course but didn't have the massive hype of say London or New York. Perfect really for a debut. The other advantage was that if something went wrong there was still the option of running Chicago a month later.

The preparations began straight away. As usual Joe wasn't slow to get things going, and just a month after Turin I went to Paris for a 15-kilometre road race and won easily in 49:17. That was a good start anyway.

In May I made the big move out of Cornafean and down to Dublin. In June I agreed to run in the Women's Mini Marathon in Dublin for the first time. It was something I wanted to do. And I enjoyed every moment of it, winning easily in 32:31, a race record. The crowds were even more incredible than I expected and I was glad to go back there for the next two years.

It turned out to be a glorious summer in Dublin, and I'm not just talking about the weather. I was spending more time with Damien. Asking him to come to my friend Deirdre Martin's wedding wasn't easy, but that was the start of the first real distraction in my life outside of running, and a good one at that.

After the wedding in the Kilmore Hotel I drove back to Dublin that night, because as usual I had a long run to do the following morning. Damien rang me the following evening. Cavan had beaten Derry in the Ulster football final that day – I had watched the game on TV – and Damien was in Cavan describing to me how the place was delirious with excitement and celebration. That gave him half an excuse to ring.

But the fact was Cavan hadn't won the Ulster title since 1969, the year I was born. In 1994, Martin McHugh took over as manager, and one of the first things he did was to bring Joe on board to help train the team. And winning that Ulster final in 1997 meant Cavan town and every other town and parish in the county went into wild celebrations. All my brothers and sisters were in Clones to witness Stephen King lift the *Anglo Celt* Cup and declare that the famine was over. I used to go to all the Cavan football matches when I was younger but once the running got more serious I didn't get to any of them. The last time I saw Cavan play was the 2001 Ulster final which they lost to Tyrone.

Anyway, Damien called again that Friday. I had only realised when I asked him to Deirdre's wedding that he was born and bred only a mile up the road in Castleknock, so we didn't have much excuse not to meet up more often after that. He was working and living in Cavan, but he made it to Dublin about twice a week.

I hadn't done any socialising whatsoever in Dublin up to that point. The truth is I just didn't know anybody. But then I met Gerry Carr and the other lads from Civil Service and started joining them for training runs. That worked out great, and I was soon running most weekends with Gerry's group out at Malahide Castle.

It was around that time I also got to know Dave and Tina Corcoran, who were both massage therapists and offered to help me out whenever I wanted. Dave was part of that group of runners out in Malahide Castle, and I always enjoyed that training environment. Not too stressful, and certainly no egos floating about.

They weren't afraid to slag me off about being from Cavan, and I liked that. At first I had a hard time understanding the strong Dublin accents, but typical of me, I was too shy to ask anyone to repeat what they said. I would just nod politely and say yeah.

Is it true that copper wire was invented by two Cavan men fighting over a penny? Yeah, that's right. Yeah.

There was a lot of slagging and joking and they treated me like anyone else. In time I became well fit for all their Cavan jokes, and certainly I found myself getting more relaxed and chatty in company – company I never had when running alone in Cavan.

Joe would come down to Dublin only about once a week, or even less. The fact was I was seeing less and less of him, and I did very little of the bounding exercises that summer. We were on the phone most days, but I knew his philosophy was that I should still be training alone, so I certainly didn't mention Gerry and the lads to him. He knew from the training and the races that I was progressing, and that was the most important thing to him.

But I still had all the self-motivation I needed, and the fact is I found the marathon training relatively easy. I had a great base built up from all the steady training over the years, going right back to my school days, and I had no problem pushing it up to 110 miles a week.

The training routine itself was straightforward. Sunday was either the first day of the week or the last day of the week, depending which way you wanted to take it. And that would usually involve a two-and-a-half-hour run. In other words about 22 miles.

On the Monday I would run 50 minutes before breakfast, which was designed to get the body used to burning fat as energy. In the afternoon I would run another 40 minutes and include some strides, such as 20 times 60 metres.

Tuesday involved one of the main sessions of the week. At the start of the summer it might be five times seven minutes, and I'd build up to five times nine minutes. Or else something like three times 15 minutes. They were always done faster than race pace.

On the Wednesday I'd just run 50 minutes in the morning and 50 minutes in the evening, and that counted as a sort of recovery day. Thursday involved another long interval session, or else repeats of 1,000 metres on the track.

On Friday I would do one long run of around an hour. And I would finish it all off on Saturday with a one-hour threshold or tempo run, which was done slightly under race pace.

Including the various warm-ups and warm-downs I'd easily clock up over 110 miles. It was intense, but I had enough time on my hands to make sure I'd recovered properly as well. Of course that just didn't leave much time for anything else.

One of the biggest tests for Berlin was going to be a half-marathon, my first ever 13.1-mile race, which was set for Glasgow on August 24th. I probably ran a little too cautiously, but I won easily enough in 69 minutes flat.

What I remember about that day was that Cavan were playing Kerry in the All-Ireland football semi-final. Unfortunately they were beaten, and my victory was little consolation to anyone back home.

I had one more race planned before Berlin and that was 10 kilometres in Perivale, in west London. I won easily in 31:21.

Just as with most of my cross-country preparation it looked like everything had gone to plan. I did one last test on the treadmill in Trinity, and they reckoned I was in the best shape of my life.

Still, Joe and myself agreed I needed to run cautiously. So much can go wrong in the marathon. I'd had problems with blisters before, and a tiny blister in the early miles could suddenly become a problem, then a big problem. I had practised taking the carbohydrate drinks, which I'd take every fifth kilometre, but I didn't know how the body would react in the heat of battle. So we were thinking of a time somewhere around two hours and 25 minutes. That would be a very respectable debut.

The plan was to sit in until 20 miles, and if I felt good at that stage then I could start racing. Approaching the 20-mile mark there were about five leaders left, including Madina Biktagirova of Belarus, Marleen Renders of Belgium and Obata Koyoko of Japan. I remember we hit a small bit of a hill and I just decided to go for it. Six miles to go, sure that was nothing. I'd run that before breakfast any morning. And I didn't even pass a wall, let alone hit it.

I'll never forget those last six miles. It felt so, so good, so, so easy. Like anyone running a first marathon I hadn't been sure if I'd even finish the thing. There had been plenty of days in the previous weeks when I thought I mightn't do it. So it was great to get through it with such enjoyment. It was a beautiful day and a beautiful course. That old saying about your first marathon being your best marathon certainly seemed to be true.

I just coasted through the finish line and glanced up at the clock: 2:23:44 – and it felt so easy. I'd run the first half in 72:42 and the second half in 71:02.

I was delighted with the time but only realised a while later that it was the fastest debut ever by a woman. And it made me the eighth-fastest woman in history. That time also fairly well destroyed the Irish record of 2:28:07 that Carey May had set back in 1985.

The world record at the time was the 2:21:06 that Ingrid Kristiansen of Norway had run in London, also in 1985, and I did wonder for a few weeks after Berlin if I could have beaten that had I really gone for it. Considering how good I felt and the good conditions I believe I probably would have broken it. Especially considering how easily I recovered. I remember John Treacy telling me I'd be coming down the stairs on my backside for the next few days. So I was waiting to wake up the next morning and needing to be lifted out of the bed. But I had no problems at all.

When I got back to Dublin the following morning I went out for an easy jog. Joe said I should just try to run maybe 30 minutes, and the legs were fine. I was so, so fit then, it was really no different from doing a hard training session.

There was only a small Irish contingent in Berlin. My other brother Seán and his wife, Elizabeth, had travelled over, and of course the ever-loyal Seán Callan and Harry Gorman. Many of the journalists weren't there for the simple reason it clashed with the All-Ireland football final, which Kerry won.

A few of us headed off to one of the Irish bars in Berlin that night where we met a large contingent of Australian runners including Shaun Creighton, one of their great distance runners. I got to know Shaun quite well over the years and he was funny and great company on a night like this.

By then most people associated a big city marathon win with a big payday. And there's no doubt Berlin was the biggest payday of my career so far. For a start I collected $40,000 in prize money plus bonuses. That was nice. I also heard afterwards that Berlin used also give a brand-new Mercedes Benz to the winner, and that was the first year they dropped that deal. That wasn't so nice.

Some people always think I'm giving them a short answer when I'm asked about the money I was making around that time. But I could never put a figure on it and say I earned this much in Berlin or that much in another race. And some people will never understand when I say money was not the motivating factor. Even if I never made one penny I still would have run.

From the very beginning I was motivated to run, not to make money, and that never changed. When the money did start coming it was nice to get it and I certainly wasn't going to turn down too many good offers. But it was never a big deal for me.

Even when I left my job in Cavan I wasn't thinking about making more money from running. I probably would have taken the time off then anyway. All I wanted to do was win. And more importantly I wanted to train hard and stay free of injury. That old saying about your health being your wealth, I love that phrase. I wish I had made it up, because I totally believe it.

I was also very lucky that people came on board to support me so early on. I suppose I did stand out because of the fact I came from such a small, out-of-the-way place as Cornafean, and through the help of people like Peadar and other family and friends I was always well looked after. Things such as a car, which I was given the use of quite early on from Brady's garage, and then other personal sponsorships from people like Boxmore Plastics, then HKM Milling, and then Kingspan and Jackson's Garage and others.

By the end of 1992 Peadar was looking after a lot of those sponsorship deals and effectively became my manager in the process. Around then I was getting most of my running gear from Reebok through Jim Kilty, one of the top running coaches. Then in 1995 I signed a much bigger deal with adidas. That was renewed three years later and they were so good to me over the years. We still have strong links today.

Paul Maloney is the head man in adidas Ireland, and he has given me fantastic support over the years, though he's never afraid to slag me off either. Paul is from Cork but whenever he rings me he puts on this thick Cavan accent. Do I really speak like that?

Athletics in the late 1980s and early 1990s was right up there in terms of the money you could make. Now most other sports have just rocketed ahead, especially soccer. I find it outrageous when I read about how much soccer players earn today.

In athletics there was certainly big money to be made on the track, but there was also good money in cross-country then. The appearance money grew over the years too, even in places like Mallusk and Dunleer. You could almost name your price there because they were very keen to have you. The only one that didn't pay an appearance fee was Acoteias in Portugal, but that was only because there was huge prize money.

Between the sponsorships and everything else it came to the point where I almost didn't have to pay for anything. That was a little embarrassing. Any time I was back in Cavan people would just hand me stuff. Even when it came to buying things like vitamin and iron supplements the local chemist would never charge me. I just wanted to pay for the stuff like everybody else. Even the testing in Trinity cost nothing because they were glad we were using their service.

On the other hand, I never applied for the Government sporting grants all during that time.

Still, when I started running the marathon the money really heated up. The fact I'd won so well in Berlin meant my stock did rise substantially. A week later I was on the *Kenny Live* television show and that's when more people started to realise I'd hit the big time and the marathon was now my main business.

Peadar and Ray were already doing some negotiations behind the scenes, and by the start of November I was signed up to run in London. I actually had nothing whatsoever to do with that deal. And I'd actually signed up to run the next two London marathons. Peadar and I headed over to meet the race organiser Dave Bedford and stayed in a big hotel beside Buckingham Palace. We were literally treated like royalty. This was the beginning of my days as one of the best marathon runners in the world.

There is big money to be made in that position, because all the big city marathons want to outdo the others in getting the best runners. But I've no idea exactly what I got to run London in 1998. It wasn't like I was the one sitting down to do the negotiations. It was more like the Catherina McKiernan team. Peadar would discuss the business end of things with Ray. Joe would discuss the racing end of things would both of them. Eileen was the accountant so she sorted out the financial end of things, and my other sister Dympna worked in the bank so she looked after the account. Of course I could trust them all, so the only thing I ever did was run.

And when the money did start coming in it wasn't like I wanted to rush out and book some lavish holiday or some fancy car. I've always had simple tastes in life and nothing about the money I earned changed that. What I did do was take advice and invest wisely. As well as property in Dublin, I invested in a couple more around the country, and luckily at the right time. They're all products of the money I earned from running.

So I got stuck into the training for London without once thinking about the money I could earn. Joe and Ray started laying down a programme of races and reckoned we should take in a few cross-country events, but the only definite plan for now was to take in altitude training at some stage before London. The only problem with that was I probably wouldn't be able to run the World Cross Country.

After just a week or two of easy running I was straight back into the hard training. I didn't realise it at the time but my body needed a much longer break than that. Just six weeks after Berlin I ran a 15-kilometre road race in Amsterdam and won it in 48:30, which was a world best at the time. Two weeks later I ran a 3.3-kilometre race in Barcelona and won that in 10:24. And another two weeks after that I ran a six-kilometre race in Palermo and won that in 18:30. It looked like I couldn't put a foot wrong.

The plan then was to run some cross-country races after Christmas, before I started into the heavy marathon training at altitude. First up was the Durham cross-country, the traditional start to the New Year, on January 3rd, which the BBC were showing live. They pulled together a very strong field, including Paula Radcliffe, and before long the BBC had billed it as a head-to-head – Paula against me. The course was very wet and muddy, which probably wasn't going to suit, but I got myself in front and went on to win it. I know Paula was sick going into that race and had to drop out but it was clear I had lost none of my ability to beat the best on the cross-country circuit.

Two weeks after that I won my second cross-country race, in Paris, and from there it was back home and the Rás na hÉireann in Dunleer on February 1st. It was one of those glorious winter days in Ireland, with clear blue skies and beautifully crisp, fresh air. There were a few other decent runners in the field but I just took off from the gun and must have won by nearly two minutes. I was flying that day. Everything about that race felt so effortless and enjoyable. The course was dry and fast and I could almost feel the breath of the crowd on my back as they shouted me on.

I remember being overwhelmed by crowds of young autograph hunters that day so much so that I took refuge in RTÉ journalist Greg Allen's car. He whisked me away so I could get my all important warm down. I later returned to the course so as not to disappoint the fans.

Days like that are what you train for – when you know you're so absolutely on top of your running that nobody can beat you. All the family were there to see it too, and it will always stand out as one of those days when running brought total contentment.

There was only one problem. I'd just run three of my best cross-country races in a long time, and that raised the obvious issue of the World Cross Country, which was set for Marrakech in Morocco at the end of March. The media picked up on that straight away and were asking me would I consider it. Deep down I wanted to say yes. They knew I had a great chance of winning it and so did I.

We felt I couldn't do both and at the time that seemed like the right decision. We'd planned on running a half-marathon in Lisbon on March 15th, which was a big part of the build-up for London on April 26th, and immediately after that heading to Albuquerque for three weeks' altitude training. The World Cross Country was on March 21st. To run that would have completely disrupted the plan. It was a tough decision, especially since I'd been preselected to run in Morocco.

In the end we had to make a decision and when I think back now it was possibly the wrong one, because I believe I could easily have done both. Paula Radcliffe has proven since that running the World Cross Country doesn't do the marathon any harm. In 2002 she won the title in Leopardstown, just a few weeks before winning in London.

But we stuck to the plan. We headed to Lisbon for the half-marathon, and I won that in 67:50, a course record and another Irish record. Again I felt unbeatable. The half-marathon is the best indicator of marathon shape, and the 67:50 roughly translated to world-record pace. I was going so well that the race highlights were shown on television at home that night.

From there we took the long-haul flight to Albuquerque via Atlanta and Dallas. Noel Berkeley travelled with us too because he was also training to run in London. After a day or two to get over the flight we got down to the hard training and had our first major session planned for the Saturday morning – the same day, ironically, as the World Cross Country. We were up shortly after seven as usual, and Noel got busy with the jumbo oat flakes to make the porridge.

Just after breakfast we realised the World Cross Country would be over in Morocco by now. I decided to call home to see how it went. I knew Sonia O'Sullivan was running but no one really expected her to feature. She'd had another disappointing summer in 1997 and had gone to Australia for the winter hoping to put her career back on track.

My mother answered the phone at home and told me Sonia had won. I got an awful jolt, a reaction I never expected I would have to news of another Irish person winning. It just hit me. I wasn't expecting it to hit me like that because I am not an envious person and I always loved to see Sonia and other Irish runners win wearing the green, white and orange.

But to hear that Sonia had won bothered me. I'd run the World Cross Country nine times and finished second four times in succession. The first year I decide not to run it, Sonia wins. I was gutted. A part of me was delighted for Sonia, but I knew I had made a huge effort to win that title over the years and had come up just short. I think it was only natural to feel a little upset. It was a crazy mix of emotions.

For the first and only time in may career I did feel Sonia had stolen some of the limelight from me, and not even in the same race. Here we were thousands of miles apart and I was upset that she'd beaten me to something. She had become first Irishwoman to win the World Cross Country. I could never beat that.

Noel was straight in with the consolation. He is naturally optimistic about everything in life. He never worries about things and has a lively sense of humour. I quickly snapped out of it, felt delighted for Sonia and focused again on the work I was here to complete.

An hour later we were on the road doing a hard tempo run and naturally I had a little bit more adrenaline than usual. By the time we got back from that run I was over what happened in Morocco. I knew my own plans were going exactly the way I wanted, and the fact Sonia had won the World Cross Country made me even more determined to win in London. From that moment on I was going to win no matter what and complete a great year for Irish athletics.

Sonia went out the following day and won the short-course title as well, which the IAAF had introduced that year for the first time. So she was actually double champion. She was obviously back to her old best.

Everything about the training in Albuquerque went to plan. Noel was good company and I enjoyed that trip more than any other.

Just before coming home I went down to Mobile, Alabama, for a 10-kilometre road race and won handily in 32:10. After that I knew all I had to do was stay healthy and I'd win in London.

I was never convinced that the altitude training made a huge difference. The few times I did try it I didn't find it any great benefit. It did make you a little more focused and got you away from distractions, but what I also found was that about four or five weeks after you came back you'd feel awful, as if the body was changing back. But at least by going away at the time we had missed some of the worst of the winter weather in Ireland.

When I got back to Dublin it seemed everywhere I turned I saw these pictures of me advertising Flora margarine, the main sponsors of the London marathon. Peadar had spotted an opportunity and agreed a separate deal with Flora, where I would front a billboard campaign in Ireland based around the London marathon. A winning combination was the slogan. I was embarrassed enough as it was whenever I was recognised out running. Now there were days when I'd be running past people at bus shelters or outside shops, and they'd look at me and then look at the posters. Another day I ran past a poster with a moustache and glasses scribbled on it, which was completely mortifying, but I couldn't help laughing at it.

But if there was pressure on me to win in London I didn't feel it. The training had gone so, so well that something would have to go seriously wrong for me not to win. Every day I went out I felt like a million dollars. All the tests in Trinity proved I was in the best shape of my life. I had already passed up on the opportunity to win the World Cross Country and there was no way I would miss the opportunity of winning the London marathon. I was going to win, and if people wanted to talk about a world record it didn't bother me.

CHAPTER 11
ON THE ROAD AGAIN

IF THERE WAS ONE RACE IN MY WHOLE CAREER WHERE I WENT TO the starting line knowing I would win, it was the London marathon in 1998. My mindset going into that race was the perfect blend of self-confidence and determination. The training had gone superbly well so I knew it was going to take someone very, very special to beat me. I hadn't lost a race in almost a year. And the fact that I'd missed the World Cross Country to concentrate solely on my preparations for London completed my determination to win.

The race was set for Sunday, April 26th, and the organisers wanted me over for a press conference on the Thursday before. That would have meant three nights in the hotel before the race, and I wanted to stay in my own environment for as long as possible. So we agreed to go over on the Tuesday to do the press conference, come back that evening, and then head back over for the race on the Saturday, just 24 hours before the start. This was Joe at his meticulous best once again.

My last hard training session was set for the Sunday before, when I did a one-hour threshold run out on the Dublin-Cavan road. By threshold I mean running close to my maximum, in this case just under marathon pace. Joe wanted to make sure everything was right and arranged to take blood samples as I was running, to measure the lactate level.

Bernard Donne from Trinity College came up to Cavan for the session and brought a little device to measure the lactate while I was running. He would drive up alongside me at intervals and I would prick my finger on a blade extended out the window of the car. The tiny blood sample was then analysed by the computer. It essentially gave a read-out of how well my body was coping with the stress of fast-paced running. From the results I knew it was coping very well. That's how thorough the preparation was.

I thought I was well used to seeing big hotels but the Thistle Tower, where they set up the headquarters for the London marathon, was particularly impressive. I sat through various radio and TV interviews before the main press conference. I know I'm every journalist's worst nightmare but that's just the way I am. I don't like being in the spotlight and worse still the centre of attention at a press conference.

I tried to give the English journalists some decent stories about playing camogie in school, and Pat Spillane being my hero, but no one seemed to get that. Paul Kimmage was one of the Irish journalists present, and he came up afterwards asking for another interview. I didn't know him at the time, but I thought we'd had the press conference over with, the questions went around to everyone, and he sat at the back and didn't open his mouth.

It irritated me that he did not ask a single question during the main press conference. He could even have asked something that might have interested the other journalists and helped them get more information out of me. Anyway, I just said, well, you had your chance. I wasn't trying to be smart. I didn't know who he was. But I'm sure I sounded a bit cheeky. So he went off and did a piece with Joe later that week instead.

I didn't actually mind too much talking to journalists as long as someone caught me straight after a race. I'd be on a high then. But an hour or so later I'd be gone back into my shell, and it would be a lot harder to talk. The only time I read anything about myself was when a paper was handed to me on a plane coming home from somewhere. I would buy them after a race sometimes just to see the pictures of myself, but I never enjoyed reading about myself.

Damien, Ray Flynn and I left Dublin early on the Saturday morning and flew to London. From the moment I stepped off the plane it was royal treatment once again. First port of call was the BBC television studios, where Brendan Foster did a 10-minute interview with me. Damien was there too and was in his element about being in the same studio as Gary Lineker and Trevor Brooking, who were doing *Football Focus* just a few feet away. Damien grew up watching *Football Focus* on BBC and I don't think he could quite believe he was now watching it live on the actual set.

Suddenly it was one o'clock and I was on the verge of starvation, the last thing you want to be the day before a marathon. Ray Flynn mentioned this to Brendan Foster and he recommended a restaurant close to the BBC studios. That will do nicely, I thought, and as usual asked for a plate of plain pasta. Not for the first time, my order met with a strange look from the waiter, and when the plate arrived it came with some kind of sauce on it. Not wanting to offend Brendan, and obviously in need of food as soon as possible, I cleaned the plate. I remember thinking at the time that the sauce tasted like it came out of a packet, but I didn't give it another thought for the rest of the day.

I never had much problem getting a good night's sleep before a major race, and the London marathon was no different. Except I had to set the alarm for 5.30, exactly four hours before the start, to give myself time for breakfast. As usual that meant a few slices of the trusted brown bread, a banana and a glass of a carbohydrate drink. I lay down for another half hour or so and then headed down to the hotel lobby to get the 7.30 shuttle bus out to the start.

While waiting for the bus I got to see my main rivals for the first time. Joyce Chepchumba of Kenya was one of the other favourites and got to wear number 101, which traditionally goes to the defending champion. I was wearing number 102. Liz McColgan of Scotland was another former winner and was still one of the toughest runners around. Marleen Renders of Belgium had recently won the Rotterdam marathon and was there too, as was Marian Sutton, who had won the Chicago marathon twice. Each of them probably believed they would win just as much as I believed I would.

I met Ray in the lobby and he seemed a lot more on edge than I was. Joe had arranged to get out to the start with me and then follow the race in one of the lead trucks.

The London marathon was one of the few races I remember watching on television as a youngster, but I never once dreamed about winning. This didn't feel like a date with destiny or my chance to become one of the marathon greats of our time. It was really just another race for me.

As usual for a big city marathon, the organisers had brought in a few pacemakers to ensure a fast time. But they went out a little too quick and I was in no rush to go with them, and neither were McColgan and Chepchumba. Two runners that did get away were Mexico's Adriana Fernandez and Romania's Lidia Simon, both very capable of winning. For a good while though, I was happy to run with the main group, thinking those up ahead were going too fast to hold on.

Then at around 15 miles I started to feel a rumbling in my stomach. Our pace was a little slower than planned early on and at first it felt like the carbohydrate drinks were building up in my stomach because of that. Then I started thinking about that pasta sauce I'd eaten the day before. Oh no, what could it be? Something in there wasn't agreeing with me.

For the next mile the cramping got steadily worse. I realised I had two choices: I could pull over to the side of the road and pray I might find a toilet or I could just keep going and pray nature wouldn't take its course. Before I had a chance to make up my mind, nature made it up for me.

Embarrassing as it was, there wasn't one moment when I considered stopping. At that stage I was just hoping the television cameras would stay in front of me and not get any close-ups from behind. I just cursed the pasta sauce for a couple of minutes and strode on.

I'd had a few minor problems with my stomach on long runs before but nothing like this. But it's part of marathon racing. I heard afterwards that Steve Jones had a similar problem when winning London in 1985. And we saw it again in the 2005 London marathon when Paula Radcliffe had to make a brief stop to answer the call of nature.

I cursed that pasta sauce one more time. But there was only a small moment of panic. Once nature had unkindly taken its course the cramps more or less disappeared. More importantly, the legs still felt fine.

At 16 miles word came back that the two leaders were 95 seconds ahead. That's a considerable lead with just 10 miles to run. And it was then that Liz started telling me I'd better go after them if I wanted to catch them. She was struggling with the pace and apparently having stomach problems of her own.

So I took her advice and started the chase – and within the next mile or so I could see Fernandez and Simon just a few hundred yards up the road. Sixty seconds became 40 seconds and then 20 seconds. I dropped one of the fastest miles of the race, 5:15, and that brought me right up to them at mile 21.

I took a quiet glance at Fernandez and could tell straight away she was finished. Within a few more strides I was gone past them both and all I had to do then was hold on. I was bouncing off the road just like another training run. I could hear the shouts for Liz McColgan back the road but there was no way she was going to have the speed to catch me.

There is no better feeling in running than coming into the final miles of a major marathon knowing you are going to win. I got that feeling in Berlin and was having it again in London. With about two miles to go Joe suddenly jumped out from the side of the road and ran along with me for a stride or two. Lets go, he shouted. He'd obviously seen enough from the lead truck, and this was his way of saying I'd won, now finish it off in style.

I had my own theory about the last miles of a marathon. The quicker I run, the sooner I'll be finished. So I ran those last two miles as fast as I could.

As the crowds thickened even more and I turned into the famous final stretch down The Mall my first feeling was relief. Just like it was when I'd run well in the World Cross Country. I had got to the stage where winning was a formality. I was at my peak, 28 years old and in the prime of my health. I'd fully expected to win and was just relieved that I did.

As usual I glanced up at the clock coming through the finish – 2:26:26. Nothing wrong with that, I thought, considering the obstacle I'd met along the way. Most of my family, including my mother and father, had travelled over and I could hear them shouting at me from the VIP stand. I was more concerned about concealing the embarrassing aftermath of the stomach cramps. I asked one of the finishing officials to get me a towel and get it quick. Then I was handed one of the large foil sheets they give you to keep you warm, but instead of throwing it over my shoulders I quickly wrapped it around my waist. Now I could go about waving to the crowd.

For the rest of that day I was on an absolute high. The winner's prize was $55,000, plus the usual bonuses, but to me that was just more money in the bank. I would have got just as much satisfaction out of winning London if there wasn't a penny in prize money. Winning was all I cared about.

About a half an hour after finishing I was handed a mobile phone. President Mary McAleese was at the other end of the line to congratulate me. Her husband, Martin, whom I got to know through running, also had a few words of congratulation. It was very thoughtful of them to call and made the occasion ever more special.

I also met Sonia later that evening when she dropped into the Thistle Tower. She'd followed the whole race from the press room. She said well done, and I congratulated her on her wins in the World Cross Country, the event I'd sacrificed to win the London marathon.

By the end of the day it had begun to sink in that I'd won something big. The London marathon was an event the whole family used to watch on a Sunday morning after Mass. Now they were all there to see me win it, except for Seán, who had to stay home and mind the farm. Giving the family that thrill was one of the main reasons I was running these big races in the first place, and London was a particularly special moment.

So much of the satisfaction I got from winning was seeing other people, and in particular my family, enjoy the moment. I remember saying that to Joe once, that I just wanted to win for my family and neighbours. And he couldn't understand that. You're joking me, he said. But that was the truth.

London brought that satisfaction more than any other race. I remember hearing from my Aunt Annie Fleming, who lives in Nottingham, that people were congratulating her at Mass the following Sunday, people who hardly knew her. I got a great kick out of that. Back in Coronea, Fr McGoldrick said the 10 o'clock Mass in a record 20 minutes so everyone could get home to watch the race. And in Killeshandra, Fr Hurley was apparently keeping people informed of my progress during 11 o'clock Mass. Shortly after Communion he announced that I'd won, and everyone broke into a round of applause, when they were supposed to be deep in prayer. I got a great kick out of that too. I also heard there were people sitting outside the church listening to the race on the radio.

I think I also realised in London that no matter how well I looked after myself, I wasn't going to have too many days like this. In a strange way I felt that winning it once was all I needed to do. At no stage in my career did I feel running was about winning titles. Winning London was never something I dreamt of. The profile meant nothing to me. I loved the winning feeling, but no more than the feeling of preparing to win. And all through my career I never wanted to race unless I was properly prepared

Over the years I've got to appreciate that victory in London more and more. In April of 2005 I was invited back for the 25th-anniversary race, where I got to meet almost all the former winners. I didn't fully appreciate it at the time, but being with all those former champions certainly made me realise how important it was to win London. Many great runners have tried to win the London marathon and never did, and after a very enjoyable weekend celebrating the 25th anniversary I knew in my heart that the Past Winners club in London is a great club to be part of.

Still, as with most of my running career, the marathon was something I more or less drifted into. I wasn't fulfilling any major ambition by winning in London or anywhere else. It wasn't a personal mission. If anything it had become more like a job at that stage. I just found myself in the situation where I had everything in place around me: sponsors, coaches, agents, everything like that. So I couldn't stop even if I wanted to. I will always appreciate my success in London.

I loved to run long before any of the success happened. The running brought me out of my shyness to a certain extent, but it brought on new burdens of its own. The more successful I got, the more trapped I felt – that I had to keep going now, try to win this or that, because I was on a roll now and, like anyone will tell you, you don't stop rolling the dice when luck is on your side. So no sooner had I won in London than all thoughts switched to the next obvious target: breaking the world record. Expectations were at an all-time high now.

Ray kicked into action straight away and went looking for the best deal around. Obviously my stock had risen even higher after London, but there were really only two options when it came to serious world-record attempts: Chicago, and Amsterdam.

Chicago was a slightly more favourable course, but the Amsterdam organisers were putting up a world-record bonus of $500,000. Obviously that helped close the deal. But the other big advantage about Amsterdam was that it was so near home that I didn't have to worry about the travelling or any major time changes. And so November 1st was circled in the running diary.

There was some talk in the media about me running the European marathon championships in Budapest in August, or even the 10,000 metres. But I did not see anything to be gained by that.

I managed to recover from London just as easily as from Berlin. Within two weeks I was back to my normal training routine, again without giving much thought to the recommended period of recovery.

We decided against altitude training this time and instead focused on adding more intense track sessions to help throw a greater share of speed into the mix. The first target was to win the World Half Marathon in Zurich, but unfortunately that plan hit a major snag.

Around the middle of July I got a letter from the national governing body of athletics, BLÉ. They wanted me to sign a contract confirming I would run the National cross-county the following year and also the 1999 World Cross Country, which was coming to Belfast. If I didn't agree to sign they wouldn't send me to the World Half Marathon in Zurich. Peadar, Joe, Ray and myself saw no reason why I should sign. No other Irish athlete had ever been asked to do something so draconian and I couldn't understand why they were coming the heavy with me like that. As far as we were concerned, Amsterdam was the only definite plan for the future, and we couldn't commit to anything after that. But I never worked like that anyway. What if I was injured? Would I be in breach of this contract? To me the whole thing was just bizarre.

I got on well with many of the athletics officials but I was always very independent to the point where I didn't draw down any government funding. Nor had I run in all of the European or World Championships which were under BLÉ control. That independent approach may not have gone down well with some of those in authority.

A year earlier there was talk that they would not send an Irish team to the world cross country championships in Turin which would have prevented me going. I hadn't run in the National Championships that year and despite my success at national and international level, my absence from those events was trotted out as an argument against me.

Strong pressure from media commentators changed their minds and, ironically, the team captured the bronze medal.

On this occassion we told them we wouldn't sign, and they said they wouldn't send me to Zurich. Fine, so we'll pay our own way. But they wouldn't have that either, claiming that because Zurich was an IAAF event, BLÉ had to sanction my entry. This was turning into a real standoff.

Once the media got hold of the story the whole thing blew up as some sort of sporting scandal and, in my view, BLÉ didn't win too many new friends. Broadcaster Marian Finucane dedicated her entire *Liveline* programme on RTÉ to the story and virtually all of the callers were highly critical of the stance taken by BLÉ.

It was a sad affair, and to this day I can't fully understand why they decided they were going to prevent me from going to Zurich. And, to this day, I have never heard of a sporting body asking a runner to commit to such a proposal.

Joe just told Ray to get me another race, and on the same day as the World Half Marathon I won the Route de Vin half-marathon in Luxembourg. The time I ran that day would have been more than enough to win the gold medal for Ireland in Zurich. A lost opportunity for Irish athletics and for me too.

I won again, a 10-kilometre race in Liverpool, on October 11th and now had an unbeaten run of 20 races going back to before the Berlin marathon. Once again it looked like everything was going to plan.

It does frustrate me a little bit knowing I could have won that world title in Zurich for Ireland. There was £25,000 in prize money too. Still, at the time I didn't lose five minutes' sleep over it. If that was the way BLÉ wanted to operate that was their problem, and I think by going for a different half-marathon we called their bluff.

As usual I travelled the day before the Amsterdam race. The flight was uneventful except for the landing, which because of the high winds was more like a theme-park ride. That's when I realised my biggest challenge in breaking the world marathon record was not going to be the distance, but the wind.

The forecast was for the winds to ease overnight, but when I walked out of the Okura Hotel the following morning a gust nearly blew me over. Still, I'd come this far, and there was no reason to back off the plan to at least attack the record, even if it was going to be a lot harder to break.

Tegla Loroupe of Kenya had run 2:20:47 in Rotterdam the previous April, which became the official world record, beating Ingrid Kristiansen's 2:21:06, which had stood since 1985. There was some controversy over it at the time because Loroupe had male pacemakers, which some people deemed an unfair advantage. But I certainly had no problem with that, and neither did the Amsterdam organisers.

The course itself was essentially two laps of the old city and almost entirely flat. It was miserably cold at the start, around eight degrees, but at least I had a few of the men running around me for company, because there were no other women up to running the kind of pace I needed on the day.

There are two main ways of approaching a fast time in the marathon – a negative split or a positive split. Some people believe the best bet is to go out conservatively and hope there will be enough left in the tank to sustain a quicker homeward run. That's known as the negative split. Others believe it's best to gamble on running hard for the first half and hope that will cushion against the hazards of fatigue in the closing miles. That's the positive split. But Joe and I agreed I should aim right between the two and target even splits of just over 70 minutes.

Gerry McGrath from Dundrum had agreed to help take me to the halfway stage, and he did a great job, running exactly 70:13. At that stage I was nearly 20 seconds inside world-record pace. At 18 miles I was still about six seconds inside the world record, but that's when the boat started to rock a little. By then I was more or less running alone, and I hit a particularly windy stretch after 21 miles. I just didn't have the physique to put the head down and tear into a wind like that, and about five miles from home I had dropped outside the target.

I finished in 2:22:23, exactly 96 seconds short of the world record. I was a little disappointed, but I knew I'd given it my best shot. In the end the weather got the better of me. But I was bumped further up the all-time list and was now the fifth-fastest woman in history. And that 2:22:23 is today still the fourth-fastest by a European woman, behind Paula Radcliffe, Uta Pippig of Germany and Ingrid Kristiansen of Norway.

I didn't leave empty-handed either, collecting about $80,000 between the prize money and the course-record bonus. Between that and other sponsors' bonuses it was obviously my biggest single payday to date.

Unlike in London, I didn't have one bad patch throughout the 26.2 miles in Amsterdam, and if it weren't for that wind knocking me off my rhythm in the final few miles I know that world record would have been mine. Deep down I felt I'd have to give it another go. I felt there was more in the tank.

Again there was some great support in Amsterdam that weekend. My family, Damien's family and many more friends from Cavan and Dublin flew over for the race, about 100 supporters in all. They dotted the course and I heard plenty of them cheering as we circled the city twice. Ray had flown in from the US and he followed the race in a courtesy car, giving Damien and Peadar regular updates by phone. I remember too the former Tánaiste John Wilson from Cavan was there to give me a congratulatory hug at the end of the race.

For the rest of the day I was physically fine. That night we found a little pub and restaurant to have a bit of a party. By 11 o'clock most of the Irish and English journalists had heard about it, and the place filled up pretty quickly. The post-race McKiernan party was always the one to go to. As usual, I let all the others do the singing and drinking for me. And with so many family and friends there, I stayed till well after midnight before getting some long-overdue sleep.

We'd arranged to fly out the following morning, and the only thing I wasn't happy about was a slight pain in the outside of my knee. I first felt it walking through the airport terminal and straight away thought it might be a problem.

I started back training shortly after the marathon, but within a couple of weeks the pain in the knee had grown steadily worse. I talked with Joe and Ray about it, and they figured it must have been brought on by sections of the course in Amsterdam where we had to run across tram tracks. I'd obviously done some sort of damage. Much later Ray told me the one regret he had about my career was getting me to run Amsterdam instead of Chicago. He reckoned the course in Chicago wouldn't have been nearly as hard on the legs. When I think about it now, Amsterdam was a tough-enough course.

RTÉ had shown the Amsterdam race live on the Sunday morning, partly in response to the criticism they got for not showing London live, and my victory got another huge reaction at home. I was back on *Kenny Live* the following Saturday, and the first question Pat asked was if I was disappointed at not breaking the world record and winning half a million dollars. No Cavan woman would be disappointed not to win half a million dollars, I told him. He got a good laugh out of that.

When I realised the knee wasn't getting any better I decided to take a break and see would rest sort it out. I was told I'd torn a bit of cartilage around the knee but it was nothing too serious. I was a little more concerned when it wasn't responding to rest, and a couple of days before Christmas I had keyhole surgery performed by Ray Moran, which cured the problem once and for all.

I finished off 1998 with my legs up, not being able to run, and I'm never at my happiest in that condition. But it had been a remarkably satisfying year. One of the things that caught my attention was the annual world ranking in *Track and Field* magazine, which is known as the bible of the sport. Forty international journalists submit votes, and I was voted the seventh-best woman athlete in the world, over all distances and disciplines, on the basis of my wins in London and Amsterdam. In the marathon itself I was voted number one.

So going into 1999, just a year and a half away from the Sydney Olympics, I was being rated as the best marathon runner in the world. As usual there would be people predicting an Olympic medal even at that stage, and I knew I was being mentioned. I didn't like hearing that sort of stuff because I knew the Olympics were still a long time away. A race that's a month away is a long time for me. And I never went out running thinking to myself, right, keep going at this pace and you'll be Olympic champion.

I missed most of January to give the knee time to fully recover from the operation, but when I eventually did get back running I found it very hard. A lot of my strength was gone, my stride was suffering, and everything took that little bit more of an effort.

My contract with London from 1998 was for two years, and that meant I had less than three months to prepare for the defence of my title. Eventually I got back to reasonable shape and went to Paris for a half-marathon at the beginning of March, which I managed to win in 71 minutes flat. The plan then was to up the training considerably, but I'd only have time to do three or four of my usual 23-mile runs.

The last of those runs was planned for Malahide Castle on a Sunday morning, three weeks before London. I arranged to meet Killian Lonergan, a fine club runner, who I think was trying to build for a marathon attempt himself. We ran for just over two hours and 30 minutes, and somewhere close to the end I felt my left Achilles tendon go. It was just a sudden jolt of pain, and it didn't even force me to stop, but by the time I got back to the house I was in agony.

For a few days I got all the physiotherapy a woman can get, but eventually it became clear I would need to rest. Three weeks' rest. On Friday April 2nd,

1999, I announced my withdrawal from the London marathon. For the first time since I'd sat in school as a teenager back in Cavan and been told I might not be allowed run the Irish Schools cross-country I started to cry. Running was not supposed to make you cry like this. Running was supposed to be fun, something I loved and something I enjoyed. Somewhere along the way I'd crossed a line and I didn't know if I'd ever make it back.

Running had become a far heavier burden than I ever could have imagined. I should have been able to walk away from it if I really wanted to, but I couldn't. I was in too deep. But I wanted to get well away from the country when the London marathon was on, so Damien and myself went to New York for a long-overdue break.

While we were in New York, Ray Flynn arranged for me to fly up to Toronto to see a sports-injury specialist. Suddenly I wasn't flying to places to race anymore, but to see these various specialists and surgeons. Little did I know then that this would become my routine over the next 18 months.

CHAPTER 12
ONE TOO MANY MORNINGS

IT'S NOT NORMAL TO CROSS THE FINISH LINE OF A RACE AND burst into tears. Tears of joy, perhaps, but not tears of heartbreak. I cried when I had to pull out of the London marathon in April of 1999, mostly because I felt sorry for all the people around me, and how disappointed they would feel. But when I crossed the finish line of the Chicago marathon that October I cried because I think I finally felt sorry for myself.

Not long after I first committed to the marathon I sensed it would be both the making and the breaking of me. Some people believe you can run only two or three very good marathons at best, and – allowing for a few exceptions – I believe them. The marathon is a monster that slowly eats into you and doesn't leave any leftovers.

For at least a month after pulling out of the London marathon I was extremely frustrated about how and why I was running. More than ever before I felt like I was running because I had to, not because I wanted to. There's a big difference. There was so much pressure on me now that there was no way I wanted to stop, even though a part of me definitely wanted to. Whenever anyone asked me about the injuries I would get very upset and just want to change the subject. I know they were just being polite and supportive but it was still the last thing I wanted to hear. I felt bad enough that I was letting people down, and I just wasn't used to this kind of disappointment. It was a real mental challenge, and that was very, very draining.

The saga continues: that's how I would start off my running diary some days. I'd also find myself dropping the odd line in there for motivation, things I might tear off a calendar or something. You've got to keep going to get anywhere. It's nice to be important but it's important to be nice. Things like that. Anything that caught my eye along the way.

Ray Flynn had come up with another good deal to run the Chicago marathon on October 24th. There was something like $65,000 for the winner, and I'd get $35,000 to run. I believed I was well able to run another marathon before the Olympics. If I could just get over the run of back luck there was every chance I could win again in Chicago, and that would set me up nicely for the Olympic marathon a year later.

Looking back now I know those injuries were really my body trying to tell me something. I needed a break. If after Amsterdam I had taken a few months off I might have got away with it. But as soon as I finished one race, it was straight back to training. There were days when I just should have taken some time off, gone and done a bit of shopping or something.

That's the first piece of advice I would give to youngsters now – don't be afraid to take a break. John Treacy once said to me your rest day is as important as your training day. Of course I should have had more sense myself and just taken the odd day off but I know I would have felt guilty.

But I didn't have much patience either. Sitting at home and not being able to run was something I was not used to. I wanted to be out racing. It wasn't like I was going out having a good time just because I was injured. I know most of those injuries would have cleared up with time, but I was always pushing myself to get back.

It was around that time, just when I was annoyed enough with the injury problems, that some people started questioning my decision to run the big-city marathons. I remember a couple of articles by Jerry Kiernan and Dick Hooper saying that some day I'd regret not running the championship marathons during 1997 and 1998. Both Jerry and Dick were great marathon runners in their time and they might see it that way. Maybe they regret not winning a major championship medal. But I never would. And if they understood anything at all about me then I think they would have seen it differently. I didn't lose any sleep over what they said, but I didn't like to see it either. People were forgetting I'd won four World Cross Country silver medals and a European gold medal and led the Irish team to a bronze in Turin in 1997.

I was going to great lengths to try and keep the injuries at bay. A while earlier my shoe sponsors, adidas, figured they could help out and brought me over to Belgium and filmed me on a treadmill to check my stride. They spotted a flick-out, where my foot was turning outward on impact, mainly when I was running slower. So special inserts were made for my shoes. But the inserts didn't work out for me and I never got used to wearing them.

I could wear any kind of shoes really. I just liked them to be comfortable. And simple. For my first marathon, in Berlin, I had this pair of very old racing shoes, which I always liked. In London I wore a slightly newer pair, but I still punched little holes into them just so they'd suit me a little better and my feet didn't get too warm. I'd get a little scissors and cut holes and strips in them. Ray Flynn was looking at them and didn't know what to say, and the adidas people weren't too impressed either. The Tuesday I got home there was this big box of new shoes waiting for me.

I was really struggling to get fit all during the summer of 1999, struggling with the mental strain as much as the physical strain. Very little about the preparations for Chicago went to plan. Joe and I had to head over there for a week in the middle of the summer to sign the contracts and do the usual press conference. To me it felt like an interruption to my training. This was the sort of thing that was really turning me against running. It was ridiculously hot at the time and I had to get up really early to run. Normally I wouldn't have minded that, but suddenly it felt like more hassle than it was worth.

I ran a half-marathon in Amsterdam on September 19th as part of the final build-up for Chicago and finished in 74:01, well down the field in seventh place and about five minutes behind the winner.

I did one of my last training sessions in the Phoenix Park about a week before Chicago and I was totally exhausted at the end of it. I knew that run wasn't right. It was hard, too hard to have been of any benefit. I was clearly taking more out of the tank than I should and just wasn't in control, nothing like I'd experienced before Berlin or London.

We headed out the week before the race to get the long flight out of my system. For the six nights before the race I didn't sleep well at all. Mentally I was having huge problems. There was the usual pre-race press conference, and the organisers were billing it as me against Joyce Chepchumba. She had taken my London marathon title the previous April, and they were comparing her childhood in Kenya with my childhood in Cornafean. The last place in the world I wanted to be was at that press conference.

I was incredibly anxious the night before the race. I'd run three major marathons before Chicago but I'd never experienced nerves as I did going to bed that night. I just knew my preparations hadn't gone as well as they needed to, and that's a fatal mindset going into a marathon. Really I was only half fit.

Not long into the race I realised that I didn't want to be out on the road running 26.2 miles. I managed to hold on to the leaders for about the first 10 miles, but by halfway I was starting to work way too hard. Ray Flynn was following on a bike and he realised before anyone else that I was in trouble. I had to endure another mid-race battle with the stomach cramps, but this time I managed to stop and find a toilet.

For the last few miles I slowed to almost jogging pace. I was exhausted, my body drained of all energy, as I crossed the finish line in 12th place in 2:35:51.

If I'd had any sense I would have dropped out of that race, but I didn't have much sense left. By now nothing about my running career was making much sense.

I was just a few feet past the finish line when I spotted Damien walking towards me, and with that I just burst into tears. I'd finished my three previous marathons with a big smile on my face, but this time I was crying.

Clare McNamara from RTÉ was sent out to cover the race, and we'd agreed I'd do an interview afterwards. She'd come a long way and I didn't want to let her down. I wasn't able to say much, but she seemed very understanding of my situation. She genuinely felt sorry for me too.

My body was very close to hitting break point, and the worst of the damage was already done. I'd clearly got the timing wrong, running all those marathons so close together. I was exhausted mentally and physically. Between the end of September 1997 and the start of November 1998 I'd run three hard marathons.

Straight after that I did most of the preparation for a fourth but failed to make the starting line. But I pressed on anyway and prepared again for Chicago. That was just too much. The fact is you can only train at that intensity for so long without taking a break, and I was ready for a break.

I'd planned on heading straight home from Chicago but Damien persuaded me to fly down to Miami for a few days, just to take it easy and try to clear the head a little. The morning after the race we took a limousine tour around the city of Chicago with Damien's brother Kenneth and friends Owen McConnon and Declan Woods from Cavan, who had travelled from home to support me. They were in good humour, and we had great fun telling yarns and jokes in the back of the limo. That helped take my mind off the trauma of the day before, at least a little bit.

Of course it was unbelievably hot when we got to Miami, but I still felt I had to go out running every day. I should have been resting that week. But I couldn't stop. There wasn't even a pause button. I was wrecked after that marathon, but still all I wanted to do was keep running. The drive that took me to the top was now working in reverse. It was actually hampering me. I was running scared, running for my life, but it was the only thing I knew how to do.

I wanted a break badly, but the Sydney Olympics were now on the horizon, so I knew I'd have to at least try and keep going. But running had become a burden. I actually felt like the rest of my life was passing me by. All those years of sacrifice, when there would be things going on in the family I wouldn't even be aware of – I didn't mind making those sacrifices at the time but now I did. The intensity, the travel, everything got to me. It was the beginning of the end.

I also suspected the success I'd had in the marathon was sending my career into decline. If I had run those three good marathons and left it at that I would have been more than content. I still think that when I moved to the marathon the timing was right, because I really had done all I could at cross-country and on the track. If I'd left it any longer it would have been too late. But once you start putting all those miles into your legs you can't go on forever.

For a few days after I got back from Florida I had no desire to go back into the hard training. By then it was hard just to run six miles, let alone 26 miles. The Sydney Olympics felt like a lifetime away. I just didn't feel driven towards them. Just a few years earlier I would have been willing to do any sort of training, whatever it took to get me to the Olympic Games in the best shape of my life. But I was already in the advanced stages of staleness and very close to being burnt out.

So I reopened my running diary on Monday, November 8th. I drove up to Cavan to meet Joe, and we did a bounding session on the Breffni Park pitch that night, and then I stayed over at home in Cornafean.

The following morning I went for a run around Cavan golf course and then headed back to Dublin and went for a run with Gerry Carr in the Park that evening. Here I was back in the old routine just over two weeks after finishing the Chicago marathon. What was I thinking?

Two days later I had a pain down my left leg, and I knew straight away it was from the bounding on Monday. All through those years I did the bounding I never felt sore like that. So I should have seen that flashing red light. This was a sign my body was not recovered. Typical though, I kept ploughing on. Every time I turned in the bed my legs hurt. But I stuck to the training. Emotionally though I wasn't exactly at my most stable.

That Friday I got a phone call from Ray Flynn, who said David Bedford of the London marathon had made contact with him about my running there the following April 16th. They put up an offer of $75,000 if I agreed to be on the start line. That actually got me a little excited, to think that people like Dave Bedford still believed I had what it took to compete in the elite race of the London marathon. And it helped restore a little confidence in my own ability. Even though I clearly wasn't running well, people still thought highly of me, and to hear that was far more important than any talk of money. At least now I had a target to work towards, and I felt winning London again was something well worth preparing hard for. I wrote in my diary that night that I was going to work hard towards reaching that goal.

I had about four months to train for London so there wasn't much room for any more injuries. After that I'd have about the same period again to train for Sydney. It was cutting it fine, but I had decided the training could be done, even all the bounding and the hill sessions, which weren't exactly coming easy to me any more.

At that time I used to go out to Swords for a hill circuit, which I really wasn't mad about, but suddenly I was quite determined to get back.

One day I was at home in Cornafean and told my mother how I felt the difference when I started back into the old-style training. She told me a story about the big hill at the back of the house, and how her legs were sore when she took to walking it again in recent years. Now she felt she could run up it. The moral of the story was that she was 66 at the time, and so I couldn't have any excuses. That kind of thing did spur me on.

Later that month though, I'd just finished a 90-minute run in Malahide when I felt another pain in my knee. I was up in Cavan the next day and told Joe straight away that my knee was sore and I mightn't be able to train. We sat in the car for a good while talking about what I should do. I think for the first time in my life I realised I was definitely pushing things over the top.

So I drove back to Dublin and told Damien exactly what happened. I don't think he knew quite what to say, but he was trying to be jovial and positive. It was, after all, my 30th birthday.

My running diary at that time was starting to resemble the daily chapters of a crisis. Instead of a few lines I'd be writing a whole page of often strange and depressing thoughts, which was not a good sign. Still, I managed to make it to Brussels for a 10-kilometre road race, my first test since Chicago, and I actually ran reasonably well to finish fifth.

Joe had a few intense training sessions planned for Christmas, including six times 1,000 metres on the Lanesboro track on St Stephen's Day. The morning after that I was running around Malahide Castle when I felt a sharp pain in my ankle. For heaven's sake, what else could go wrong?

The day after that I was back in Cavan for more bounding. I managed a 20-minute warm-up, but there was now a definite pain in the ankle. And as I went through the bounding it gradually got worse.

I was just praying that a couple of days off would get rid of this, but something inside told me it was going to be a lot longer.

The first thing I had to do was cancel my run at the Mallusk cross-county in two days' time, the first cross-country race of 2000, and that's when it really hit me. I cried that night like I'd never cried before. It wasn't just about missing Belfast. I had wanted to show people I was back in form.

The next day Damien got Ger Hartmann on the phone, and he agreed he'd see me first thing in the morning. Damien and myself hit the road early on

Saturday morning, and halfway to Ger's clinic in Limerick we got a call from Greg Allen of RTÉ radio. He was on his way to Belfast, like everyone else, and wanted to know why I wasn't going. It was hard for me to tell him why I couldn't be there, but he himself seemed quite down about it and sympathetic.

Ger checked out the ankle and recognised what the problem was: a stress fracture. Still, he didn't want to rule anything out, so he arranged for me to have an X-ray.

Damien and I checked into Jurys for the weekend. After dinner we headed out to a local pub. It was a dark, wet afternoon in Limerick and Munster had just won a European Cup rugby match. Most of the team and coaching staff and a good few supporters were in the pub. It was a lively spot. Declan Kidney, the coach, and Mick Galwey, the Ireland international, came over to say hello. I managed a smile and congratulated them. Little did they realise what I was going through.

On the Tuesday I went for a more thorough bone scan and then got the news I'd expected. Ger called it a greenstick fracture of the lateral malleoli. Better known as a fracture of the ankle bone. The strange thing is the news didn't hit me that badly. I was upset, even a little angry, yet there was almost a sense of relief as well.

But this hardship just didn't seem worthwhile. Not even the best days could make up for it. If I'd backed off a little earlier I could have prevented this. If I had stopped after Amsterdam in 1998 for even a couple of months I'm sure I would have avoided it.

All I wanted to do then was get back to a level of fitness where I could at least run pain-free. As winter gave way to spring 2000, I was spending most mornings in the pool, but I rarely thought about making it back for the Sydney Olympics. I just wanted to get on with my life. I remember in April I went shopping in Grafton Street with Dympna, Eileen and Rose. I also started doing some decorating in my house in Dublin, another sign I wasn't willing to put everything into running anymore. I never would have done that before.

It was in that frame of mind that I made my decision to pull out of the Sydney Olympics. I knew I had no chance of getting the motivation back. Even when I managed to get back running my diaries were full of negativity. I didn't mind the disappointments of a race or a session as long as I could go out running the next day, where I could always forget. If I couldn't go out running, those disappointments would linger.

I laugh when I read those diaries now, but at the time every one of those emotions was real. I was actually angry for allowing myself to get so depressed over my running. I could just about handle the injuries, but I didn't like telling people I wasn't running.

Getting on with my life had taken me as far away from running as I'd ever been. Marriage would be the first step, and starting a family would be the second. Suddenly these were the only things that mattered to me. For the first time in my life I put my love of running on hold, and with that my running career on hold. And deep down I did wonder if I'd ever get it going again.

CHAPTER 13
RESTLESS FAREWELL

IT WAS TWO YEARS AFTER THE SYDNEY OLYMPICS BEFORE I rediscovered my desire to put running back to the forefront of my life. For two years I didn't know and didn't really care if I'd ever compete again on the world stage. Some days I'd feel like I'd done it all and should retire. Other days I'd be out in the Phoenix Park doing an easy run and suddenly I'd feel this great desire to get truly fit again.

I'd go days without thinking too much at all about running, especially when I was pregnant with Deirbhile, who was born on March 7th, 2002. Childbirth killed off that competitive streak – at least temporarily.

I knew I'd always have the desire to run again, but there's a big difference between running an easy 50 minutes every day and doing the hard, intense training necessary to run competitively. But by the end of August 2002 I felt I was ready to at least start the journey.

It was Damien who actually coaxed me into ringing Joe Doonan again. The truth was I'd got myself reasonably fit since giving birth to Deirbhile, and if I was going to give the running another go it was more or less now or never. But I had only very vague thoughts about giving it another go for the Athens Olympics, which was exactly two years away.

I took a long time thinking about it, but one day I plucked up the courage and rang Joe's house. I wanted to begin the process of putting together a team and a structure that would help me make a strong comeback. It was the first time I had spoken to Joe for many months.

We talked for no more than three minutes, and he asked me to leave it with him. About a week later he rang back and agreed to come to the house. We had a good long chat. He was trying to assess my commitment. Eventually we decided we'd at least give it a try.

Joe worked out the drill. On Tuesdays and Thursdays I would go to Virginia, about a 70-minute drive from the house in Castleknock. I wasn't too keen on that idea considering I had a six-month-old baby to look after, but Joe felt it wasn't going to work out unless he saw me run at least twice a week.

We'd meet at the Ramor United football grounds, where there's an all-weather track of 300 metres. I would arrive at 4.00pm and by 4.30pm I'd be warmed up and ready to go and the training would last until 6.00pm. It was rough going but I agreed to try it for a couple of months. Joe also agreed to come down to the Phoenix Park on a Saturday morning to watch me do a threshold run, or whatever training he had planned for me.

At first I would just do a few drills along with the running. By November I was back doing the bounding exercises. Not as intense as when I was a 20-year-old, but still intense enough to cause some problems. Here I was – a few weeks short of my 33rd birthday and with a baby daughter at home – up in a football field in Virginia doing high kicks and pogo jumps. But it was my choice. This was what had to be done if I was going to get back to real racing fitness.

Around that time I brought Anthony Geoghegan up to meet Joe in the house in Castleknock. Dave Corcoran had put me in touch with Anthony's physiotherapy clinic in Carlow, and straight away I reckoned he was one of the best around. He was fantastic with injuries but also with general maintenance. Even when I was pregnant he gave me lots of exercises and stretches to make sure my back stayed strong. Anthony was the one man I went to who actually got to the root of the problems. He was very knowledgeable and I had great trust in him.

I know Anthony was the main reason I was able to get back running so soon after giving birth.

I wanted to build a team of people around me, something like Paula Radcliffe had done with Ger Hartmann, and I thought Anthony and Joe could work together and maybe figure out some training between them.

But the idea never made it past the drawing board and instead I continued to train with Joe and visit Anthony.

Towards the end of November I rang Ray Flynn to see what races were coming up. Ray got me a race in Ghent, Belgium, the Lotto Cross Cup, and I finished ninth. It was a typical twisty and winding cross-country course and I was in no way ready for it. It was of course a respectable run under the circumstances, but it was a rude awakening for me after so long away from racing. I'd had one small road race over the previous two years so from that point of view it was also significant.

I did an interview on RTÉ radio later that afternoon and it sounded as if I was making a big comeback. To me it didn't feel like a comeback at all because I knew I was still a long way short of race fitness and fast losing that desire to even do the hard training any more.

I wasn't enjoying the trips up and down to Cavan, leaving Deirbhile behind. There were days when my mother would have to come from Cavan to look after Deirbhile, while I drove up in the opposite direction to Virginia. And it got more and more frustrating as the weeks passed.

Ray did another deal for me and had me entered for one of the Grand Prix races, also in Belgium. I said there was no way I was going to race again so soon, forget it. I just wasn't ready. So Joe and I decided the next race would be the Belfast cross-country on January 11th, formerly staged in Mallusk but now in the grand setting of Stormont Estate. But there'd be nothing grand about my entrance there because I never got to run.

Exactly a week before Christmas my body just broke down again. I was up in Virginia doing one of the bounding sessions when I felt a pain in my right knee. It was a freezing-cold evening, and as soon as I started warming down after the training session I could feel the pain worsen. I got into the car and drove home and by the time I got to Castleknock I could hardly walk. I knew it was time to change tack. I was never going to get back competing if I stuck to this routine. I just knew that. There would have to be another way or no way.

By the end of 2002 my running career had hit another all-time low. My legs were lifeless and my whole body felt tired and weak. This was something new, because from a young age I had known how important it was to get a good night's sleep, and even when I was training at my absolute hardest I never felt I'd hit the point of total exhaustion.

I just knew I couldn't end my career like this. If I never ran another race I wouldn't have cared, but I just wanted to be able to go out and run for an hour every day, just like I'd done as a youngster. I had to get back to that point. I didn't think I'd be able to enjoy life if I couldn't.

I wanted to get strong enough again even to go out and run a few miles every day, so I went on a weight-training programme, something I'd never done in my life. But I needed to build up my upper body, because my posture was all off. I slowly built up different muscles in my back, using light weights and lots of repetitions.

The businessman Ben Dunne had given me membership of his gym in Blanchardstown, and again I was humbled by the support.

Dave set up a meeting with Emily Foster, who had done some physiological work with the Ireland rugby team, and she did various biomechanical analyses of my running style. She told me my stride had deteriorated so badly that she didn't want me to race again for at least three months.

Damien had also agreed to take time off work from January until the end of March to give me more time to train. The fact that so many people around me were so eager to help was making the hard road at least a little smoother.

By the middle of April I felt I was ready for my first test, and I agreed to run the Dunboyne four-mile road race on Easter Sunday, April 20th. All I'd done going into that race was easy running, and not one hard session, but I managed to finish third behind Pauline Curley and Annette Kealy, in 21:45. Not bad at all, I reckoned, considering all I was trying to do was run without pain.

I just wanted a race, but in a way I wanted to get beaten as well, to relieve some of the pressure. Let everyone know I wasn't going too well. Dave gave Pauline and Annette a fierce slagging afterwards. Did you enjoy that? Well it won't ever happen again.

Lindie Naughton of the *Evening Herald* was there and I told her I was going to run the Women's Mini Marathon in June – a sure sign I was on the road back.

I felt I needed some target though, and I decided the Women's Mini Marathon in June was perfect – a low-pressure 10-kilometre race I'd enjoyed on the three occasions I'd run it. I circled the date in my diary, June 2nd, and got on with the slow and painful process of learning to run all over again.

It was around that time that I last heard from Joe. Damien persuaded me to write a letter to Joe, just to explain things. The letter was really just to thank him and to explain that life had moved on; with Deirbhile on board it was just too difficult to be driving up to Virginia twice a week.

I wrote the letter and left it on the kitchen table, where it sat for weeks. I'd pass it every day and find some excuse not to post it. Eventually it found its way into the bin. I always regret not sending it.

Not long after, Joe rang the house. We talked for only a couple of minutes, because I think we both knew it was time to go our separate ways. I was a wife and a mother and settled in Dublin – all differences between now and when I started with Joe back in the early days.

I was blessed with a remarkable natural talent and Joe Doonan had shaped and moulded that talent over many years using his own special abilities.

I cannot say whether I would have enjoyed similar success had Fr Oliver O'Reilly not arranged for me to meet Joe all those years ago in 1987. What I can say for certain is that Joe's work with me led to my greatest triumphs and that his involvement was crucial in achieving that success.

I was still taking each week as it came, just trying to improve things slowly but surely. By the time the Women's Mini Marathon came around on June 2nd I'd made further progress, but I didn't go into that race with any great ambitions, mainly because Sonia O'Sullivan was there to run too. The newspapers were making a big deal of that, and how it was our first race together on Irish soil since we were youngsters. I knew I was a long way off the kind of shape Sonia was in, and she beat me by about a minute. But I was happy to finish second because it was a hard run. And like Dave had predicted, Pauline and Annette both finished behind me this time.

During the summer I ran a couple more road races, all the time thinking about having a serious go at one more cross-country season. I set myself one goal, and that was to win back the National cross-country title.

By the start of November I felt like I was very close to coming around. I was doing some decent sessions in the Phoenix Park and out at Malahide Castle, but in the week before the Intercounties cross-country I felt a slight head cold coming on. Within 24 hours I was stuck to the bed with a vicious dose of flu. For a couple of days I could barely even look after Deirbhile and had no choice but to pull out of the race.

Because I'd run well at a race in Margate in England a few weeks earlier I was still selected to run in the European Cross Country in Edinburgh in December. I should have pulled out of that race too, but I just couldn't bear the thought of letting people down again. The flu had knocked me back weeks rather than days and I went over there with little confidence. As I expected, I couldn't get going at all and ended up back in 34th. I came through the finishing chute and met Damien, and he could see the tears in my eyes.

The European Cross Country was a race I had won in 1994, and in finishing so far back I think I realised for the first time that my best days were behind me. As I headed off for a quiet place to reflect on a bad run it was announced that we had won silver medals in the team race. That was small consolation. It was very tough going. I was surrounded by lots of journalists in the mixed zone and I could tell by the way they were looking at me they too realised it was the end of my era.

Still, I'd come this far so I was determined to keep going until the National cross-country at the end of February. It was set for Roscommon racecourse and the whole family had arranged to travel to it.

The great thing is I went there believing I would win. Just like old times. It had been 10 years almost to the day since I'd won my last National cross-country title, in the Phoenix Park, and it would mean a lot to win it again.

I was so confident I just held back on the first lap and allowed Rosemary Ryan, Maria McCambridge and Jolene Byrne to run a few yards ahead. I was in total control, just like the Irish Schools cross-country all over again. By halfway I was running with them, and then I just stretched away to win easily on the last lap. I got as much satisfaction out of that victory as I did from any other major race.

Just to see the smiles on the faces of my parents again meant so much to me. My nieces and nephews and Deirbhile were also there and they had never seen me race before, and this was the complete picture of satisfaction I'd always aspired to. After the race we all headed to a pub in Roscommon owned by Séamus Duke, a very good friend of Damien's from their days working together at Shannonside/Northern Sound. We had a thoroughly enjoyable evening and I finally felt like everything I'd struggled through over the previous two years had been worth it.

The only down-side was that Damien himself wasn't there; he was in Thurles, where our local GAA club in Castleknock, St Brigid's, were playing in the All-Ireland club football semi-final. He was putting together a radio documentary charting the team's progress through the championship and had been following them for six months, so he had no option but to go to Semple Stadium. As well as that, he's a staunch club member, though given the choice, and the occasion that was in it, he would probably have opted for Roscommon.

He rang Tina Corcoran from the stand in Thurles, and Tina gave him a running commentary on the race. He was the only St Brigid's person in Thurles with a smile on his face that evening. I had won but St Brigid's had been beaten by the Kerry champions, An Gaeltacht.

A week later I went to Rás na hÉireann at Dundalk racecourse, another occasion that reminded me of the better days, and winning there again allowed me to prove to myself that I could still satisfy my own targets. Winning that race didn't do the motivation any harm either.

The World Cross Country was set for Brussels in March and I wanted to find out one more time where exactly I stood on the world stage. I'd run nine consecutive World Cross Country championships between 1989 and 1997, and I was determined to do one more. As it turned out, the course in Brussels was particularly tough, just a horrible surface to run on, and I quickly realised I wasn't up for the challenge. I didn't enjoy it and finished 30th. But I didn't regret going there because I had to find out for myself what level I was at, and obviously the writing was on the wall.

Things improved again though after that. Sonia was back in town to run the Great Ireland Run in the Phoenix Park in April, and I beat her easily that day. It was obvious she was only coming back from injury, but I still got great satisfaction from winning that race on my own doorstep, a two-minute run from the house, and with plenty of neighbours and familiar faces there to clap me home.

From there it was back to the Women's Mini Marathon, another race I wanted to win one more time, which I did. I was on such a high after it that when Tom O'Riordan and Cliona Foley of the *Irish Independent* asked me about the Athens Olympics I said I'd be thinking about it.

That was a talking point in the papers for a few weeks. I was prepared to try and get the qualifying time for the 10,000 metres, and if it happened it happened. But it wasn't something I had my heart set on. And deep down I knew the burning desire just wasn't there. I had been to two Olympics, and that had more than satisfied my desires. Yet if I had been in 31:30 shape or thereabouts I would have given the qualification time a shot and probably would have been more confident and upbeat about going to my swansong Olympics.

I went out to Santry and started doing a few track sessions. I needed to run 31:45 in order to qualify, but I struggled to get down to doing six times 1,000 metres in just over three minutes. I knew it wasn't nearly comfortable enough, and anyone could have told you that didn't translate to 31:45.

It's a huge honour to make the Irish team for the Olympics, something very prestigious and something to be taken very seriously. But in reality I was only kidding myself and everyone else by thinking I had enough time left to reach the qualification mark.

At this stage of my career there was no point in going to the Olympics just for the sake of it. I would have to be a medal contender if I was going to take my place in the Irish squad. And there wasn't an ounce of hope that I would even make the final. It was time to face the music and tell everyone I wasn't going to make the grade for Athens.

In the middle of June I announced that I wouldn't be doing any more track races. Ever. That was the end of the Athens Olympics. I know Damien was more disappointed than I was, but deep down he knew too there was just no point in going on. It was bound to happen sometime that I would hit a point where I couldn't compete at the top level any more. That's sport. That's life.

When I was in my prime on the world stage I thought I could do this forever. So what if I get old? If I keep fit it will never come to an end, I would tell myself. But sooner or later Father Time catches up.

I was still fit. I could still run 10 or 12 miles a day, and pretty fast too. But I wasn't 25 any more. I had achieved all my big international successes during a seven-year period in the 1990s. That's a pretty decent stretch of international success in any language.

Thankfully, even with the lure of another Olympic Games, I knew I had to be realistic. There are younger, faster runners coming through all the time, and no matter how I tried I wasn't going to be able to match them. But the thought of that didn't frighten me. I knew life had plenty more to offer me outside of running. It was time to face up to that, and by trying to make the Athens Olympics I would have been only fooling myself that my time at the top wasn't coming to a close.

And at no point did I even consider running the marathon in Athens. Physically I just wasn't up to it, let alone mentally. The truth is I'd developed a fear of the marathon. I only had to think about what the marathon had done to my running career, and the pain and suffering I went through in the aftermath of running three hard marathons in a year. Nothing in the world was ever going to persuade me to run another marathon. I got all the success I ever wanted in the marathon and I still appreciate all I did in the marathon. My Irish record of 2:22:23 will always mean a lot to me no matter how long that record remains.

And I am still the fourth fastest European ever to run a marathon. Apart from Paula Radcliffe no other European has run a faster marathon over the past eleven years.

I won a couple more road races in the Phoenix Park over the summer, and that satisfied whatever desire I had left to compete. Towards the end of the summer I was asked to compete in the Great North Run in Newcastle on September 26th. That was another race I'd never run and had always wanted to. I agreed to go, while half suspecting it might be my last race ever.

CHAPTER 14
A NEW DAWN

WHEN I CROSSED THE FINISH LINE OF THE GREAT NORTH RUN in Newcastle I looked up at the clock and saw 75 minutes. Normally I would look at the seconds as well, but all I needed to see was 75 minutes. That was sign enough. My time was up. In the past I had run that half-marathon distance in 67 minutes. I knew exactly what that time meant.

I had actually said to Damien the night before the race that this was looking like the end. I was two months away from my 35th birthday and I was happy to finish my last race with a smile on my face. I didn't even know or care what place I finished. It was September 26th, 2004, the day I retired from competitive running.

For the first time in my life I didn't do any warm-down after a race. I had hinted to people over the previous few months that I was thinking of retiring from competition. And I think Damien realised right then that I was totally serious about retiring. He knew there was no point in even trying to tempt me to change my mind.

I just grabbed my bag and, instead of waiting for the athletes' courtesy coach, Damien and myself headed straight for the train back into Newcastle. Later we ended up in the Irish Club near St James' Park, the home of Newcastle United

FC, watching the All-Ireland football final between Kerry and Mayo. Damien picked up a beer mat in the club and we started drafting the press release we were going to send out the following week. I was officially retiring from athletics and I was absolutely relieved. I've got a healthy body, I told him to say, and a healthy mind, and I can't ask for anything more than that.

We were both satisfied it was the right thing to do. I was glad Damien was with me on this one. He agreed that if the hunger wasn't there it would be foolish continuing. So we sat back and enjoyed the match, which Kerry won.

Then we found a nice restaurant and chilled out for the evening. Already I felt I was entering a new phase of my life, which didn't revolve solely around racing and training.

I knew there was no going back. I knew too there was no way I could go into another cross-country season. I wouldn't have got satisfaction out of winning another national title, and I knew I wasn't going to do anything on the world stage. I knew from the training it wasn't going to happen for me again. That hunger was gone. When I was younger I just loved to train hard. I had complete tunnel vision, and it was train, train, train. There was only a small percentage of that left. Maybe less than one percent.

I was also a perfectionist. I knew what was needed to get to the top, and I just wasn't prepared to do that any more. And if I couldn't do it properly I wasn't going to do it at all. I no longer had the desire to train hard, to get out twice a day in all weathers, to spend hours and days travelling to races. I wanted to leave all of that behind me and finally get on with the rest of my life.

In the months and weeks leading up to that decision I was a little worried about possible withdrawal symptoms, and if I might somehow regret it. Within a few weeks I knew there wasn't going to be any regret. Once I was still able to get out running every day I knew I'd always be satisfied.

When I called my father and mother with the news I could sense they were as relieved as I was. They didn't want to see me go through any more disappointment, and they sensed I was totally happy about what I was doing. All during my career they could tell by the tone of my voice how I was feeling. If I was down about something they would sense it straight away. If I was excited about some race then they knew I was going to win. And it was obvious that day that I was feeling perfectly content to tell them I was retiring.

They would miss some of the excitement and the enjoyment I'm sure, but they had always kept their distance from my running too and never treated me differently from the rest of the family. There were six other McKiernan children and they always got the same time and attention from my parents as I did, which was the way it should be. My running career was never allowed take over the family.

To give an example, after my London marathon win in 1998 my sister Rose got back before the rest of the family. She tidied the house and lit the fire, and my father was delighted to be welcomed home to that. He was going around that night saying Rose was the best of the whole lot of us, half joking whole in earnest, London marathon or no London marathon. All the McKiernan children were treated exactly the same, and I was always grateful they kept it that way. So they certainly didn't make any big fanfare about my retirement.

A week later Damien sent out the press release announcing my decision to retire. I took several calls that day from journalists and I must admit it was emotional talking to them about all the great times I'd enjoyed in the past. But still I didn't regret my decision in any way. I think everyone I talked to that day understood why I was retiring. At least no one else tried to tempt me to change my mind. It was still a great relief to me that I was able to put that part of my life behind me, knowing I was lucky to have achieved so much.

We finished off the press release by saying I would run a road race in Cavan on October 10th and it would be my farewell race.

That race was organised by Annalee, the running club I had joined after Cornafean AC became less active in recent years, and it turned out to be the perfect send-off. All my family and many friends and neighbours were there, just like they had been all through my career. I won that race without any regrets about my decision. And I couldn't imagine a more fitting place to say my goodbyes to competitive running.

The funny thing was I was still getting offers from the New York and Chicago marathons. New York were particularly keen and were offering me a lot of money if I would just agree to start their marathon in November. They weren't looking for me to run 2:20 or anything like that, but just to be there, to have some Irish presence. But for all the money in the world there was just no way I was going to run another marathon.

Around this time Dave and Tina Corcoran were in Canada on holidays and brought me home a present of a book: *Chi Running*, by Danny Dreyer. I'm normally a little slow getting into books, but when I started reading this one I couldn't leave it down. I was hooked. My first thought when I finished it was that I'd have to get in contact with the man. I wanted to find out more about Danny Dreyer and chi running.

So much about the book made sense to me. It was about a revolutionary new approach to effortless, injury-free running, and I believe that's exactly what chi running is. It's also what every runner wants, but I think I could probably relate to it more than most.

I practised some of the focuses and immediately found them beneficial. I'd always had tight calf muscles from pushing off with my toes rather than lifting my feet. Since learning the chi running techniques I haven't had even a minor calf-muscle problem or even a single niggle, and I still run for an hour or so every day, and some days more if I have the time.

More importantly, there have only been a couple of days since I've retired when I haven't gone running. And that was only because I was travelling all day. I haven't had one injury, and I am definite that so much comes down to what I've learnt about the chi running techniques.

I wish I had come across this at the start of my career, but as the saying goes, there's no point in living with regrets. At least now I'm able to help others try to avoid hurting themselves and run injury-free.

It was so ironic that just as I was closing one chapter in my life, my racing career, I was introduced to chi running, which opened a new one.

Within a few weeks I managed to get in contact with Danny in America, where he presents workshops in chi running. In February 2005 I went to Miami to attend one of his tutor-training courses, and after some further study I was fully certified in the teaching and methods of chi running.

I spent a lot of time in America over the first six months of the year, travelling there four times between February and June.

I've found the whole thing fascinating and feel it's worth sharing with others, because showing people how to run properly is an entirely new concept. Everybody that runs wants to enjoy it and be able to run injury-free. And that's the main aim of chi running, which is partly based on t'ai chi principles but puts the main emphasis on correct posture. If you're not running in a natural way you're going to hurt yourself, no matter how careful you are.

I definitely believe my running style deteriorated over the years. I wasn't the most economical, running on my toes too much, and my posture wasn't correct. Years ago even my father asked me why I was running up on my toes so much. My style probably looked good, but there was a lot of wasted energy. That was the only way I knew how to run.

There are so many positive elements in chi running that I want to pass the techniques on to other runners. I've set up my own teaching practice and I've really enjoyed showing people the correct mechanics for running. I've got tremendous satisfaction when people come back to me saying they can now run injury-free, because that's the whole point of chi running. It's ironic to think I'm getting so much enjoyment showing people how to run correctly after I myself spent so long injured and desperate for a cure. It's almost a vocation with me.

Running itself doesn't give you injuries, but the way you run does. If you move your body incorrectly, over time you're going to injure yourself. Unfortunately, running is associated with injury, but it needn't be if you do it properly.

So far I've had no desire to go into any formal coaching of elite runners, because I regard myself as a perfectionist and I'd expect 100 percent commitment from those I'd work with, and people with that sort of commitment are rare. But I always loved to run, and now I can at least help people that just want to enjoy running in the same way I did.

One of the things I have often said to Damien is that I probably should have enjoyed my running career a little more. I never doubted how lucky I was to carve out a career doing what I love best, despite the hard days. And I know every job has its lows as well as its highs so it probably was no different from the ups and downs I would have had in a nine-to-five job. But there were days when I was very, very down because of my running. There's no doubt about that. I would get upset about something like a calf-muscle strain or some stiffness in my knee.

That kind of thing seems so irrelevant when I think about it now. I actually can't believe I used to get so upset about having to pull out of some race or would sit at home crying if I couldn't train. If I had stopped to think about the children in hospital with some serious illness, or people with real troubles in the world, then obviously my problems would have looked tiny. But that's how caught up I was in my running and how blinded I was by my daily routine of training. If that routine was broken I felt my world was ending.

I also think I could have walked away when I was at the top, say after the Amsterdam marathon in 1998. I know athletes say the best time to retire is when you're on top, because if you've been on the road as long as I was then you're bound to fall sooner or later. I was definitely at the top after winning in Amsterdam, and things did fall to pieces quite rapidly after that.

I suffered a lot of injury towards the end of my career. I could have retired once those injury problems started – I had achieved so much in the six years before that, which was a damn good return in any sport – but I didn't see any way out of it. And I do think that after Deirbhile was born I was ready to stop running competitively. Most of the desire to train hard was gone by then.

And so I'd be lying if I said I'd do it all the same if I were starting again.

But I honestly can't have any regrets about my running. I feel I have so much to be thankful for. I know it's a cliché to say you shouldn't have any regrets in life, but as far as my running career goes I don't have any. I will always be able to count more highs than lows. There were so many great times there, and I was very fortunate to see all the things and places I did.

All I have to do is think about how far my running took me. One of the days I disliked most as a youngster was New Year's Eve, when my brothers and sisters would try to drag me out celebrating. One time they got me out on the town, and I kept asking my brother Seán to take me home. Of course he stayed longer than he normally would just to wind me up. But it wasn't my scene. So I think for someone who was that shy growing up, I didn't do badly at handling my running career at such a fever pitch.

I still run about 60 miles a week and I know that love of running will survive as long as I live. Whenever I think back on my career I do feel a strong sense of satisfaction. I know I'm lucky in so many ways to have got so much out of running. I know plenty of people have given running as much effort and time as I did and got very little out of it.

I know I'm lucky as well to have finished my career with a healthy body. If I had picked up a truly serious injury over the years that meant I couldn't go out running any more I think I would probably hold a few hard feelings. But the fact I can still run as much as I want means almost all the memories are sweet, and will always be.

I only have to think about the good times to know it was all worth it. And I'm proud of everything I've achieved in running. And when I look at my list of successes now, I realise they are the sort of successes that will not be easily surpassed by anyone else in the future.

I also know I'll never run another competitive race. I know you should never say never about anything in life, but I mean never. I'm just not the sort of person who could go back into a competitive situation like that half-heartedly. If I wanted to race again I'd feel I needed to do that hard training again, and I know that's not going to happen. I know I'll never have the ambition to do the training again, and that's why I know I'll never race again.

I'm lucky I could walk away the way I did and turn my focus to the many other things life can offer, like family and another career.

Even though I run every single day I don't ever view it as training. Some days when I'm running in the Phoenix Park the legs will feel particularly good and I'll push myself a little hard up a hill or something like that. But that's as far as it goes. There's even a big difference between training hard and racing.

I know many runners can continue to compete at some level long after they retire. But not me. I'm too much of a perfectionist to even try that. I think it would just ruin the way I feel about running now. For a start I'm a bad loser. I'd hate for any runner to beat me now, just like I did when I was at the peak of my career.

I know as well that I'd get no fun out of racing just for the sake of it. I'm still too competitive for that. It actually surprises me sometimes just how competitive I still am. There are days when I could be out on the road or up in the Park with Deirbhile and we'd be running around or whatever. She might start racing me back to the car or to the house, and the honest truth is I have a hard time letting her beat me. That's how competitive I still am. So I know if I jumped back into a race I would try to win it, and I don't want to go that road again.

One day not long after I'd retired, Damien was clearing out the garden shed and found my old skipping rope. I did a lot of skipping when I was younger and always found it a great way of improving my fitness. Damien was trying to show Deirbhile how to skip, but I then took the rope. It took me a while to get the hang of it again, and there was no way I was giving the thing to Deirbhile until I did. It sounds ridiculous but that's just the way I am.

The girls in the camogie team down at St Brigid's GAA club were asking if I would go back playing for the team, even after a 17-year gap. I'd love to give it a go sometime but I just don't have the time, and anyway I wouldn't go back unless I knew I could play as well as when I wore the Cornafean jersey. Do it right or don't do it at all has always been one of my mottos.

In many ways what I get out of running now are the same things I got as a youngster. Just being outside in the fresh air still feels as good as it did when I was a child growing up in Cornafean. Even if it's cold and wet outside I still enjoy it as much. It's also the feel-good factor of moving freely about and feeling fit and healthy. I discovered that feeling at an early age and never lost it.

The only real difference about my running now from when I was a youngster is the way I think about my style. I've been so fascinated by chi running that I think about it every time I lace up the shoes. I am now putting things right for other people, not in the sense of healing injuries, but more in preventing them. I never imagined I'd get so much satisfaction out of that, and it's opened up a whole new chapter to my running career that I'm enjoying just as much as when I was winning big races around the world.

I'll keep on running as long as I can. I won't ever need to look at the clock or worry about the distance or about who is behind me. In a strange way running feels just as important as it ever did, and yet not as important. I think all I've been through has helped me realise that running and happiness go hand in hand in my life. I don't think I could ever separate the two. So I'd like to think I could run on and on forever, a million miles and more.

CHAPTER 15
RUNNING FREE

HEADING INTO 1998 AND THE START OF MY PREPARATIONS FOR the London marathon I'd already spent almost a decade involved in athletics at the highest level. I'd run in nine World Cross Country championships, two World Championships on the track, and twice at the Olympic Games. I'd also taken my first step into the big-city-marathon circuit. At no stage during that time did I ever see evidence that any of the athletes around me were taking drugs. But of course some of them were.

The use of illegal, performance-enhancing drugs is a problem for many sports, and athletics is certainly no exception. Every now and again I'd hear rumours of drug use in athletics and it was certainly one of the regular topics of conversation during the later years of my running career. Still, all I was ever concerned about was my training and my racing, and not what some other runner might be taking.

When I first started competing in major championships I was hardly aware of the drugs issue at all. No one around me talked about it. I would look at the sprinters sometimes and wonder how they managed muscles that big, but it was never talked about in middle-distance terms.

When the Chinese runners first came on the scene in 1993 things changed.

They were known as Ma's Army. They just came out of nowhere. I couldn't figure out how anyone could do that, just turn up at a major championship for the first time and win so easily, smashing world records out of sight in the process.

None of the athletes I was running against at the time ever tested positive for anything. I know some people had some suspicions about certain athletes that ran against me, but I didn't. Things like EPO, the endurance-boosting drug, weren't even discovered in the early 1990s so it was very rare for any distance runner to test positive for anything, unlike today.

To me hard training and dedication were the only ways to succeed.

A lot of that comes down to the way I was brought up. My parents had a strong faith and passed it on to us.

I always said a prayer before a race. Even before some of the harder training runs. Just a quick blessing really, asking that I would get through it safely and not injure myself. I think that was one of the reasons I was always so calm before a race. I just wanted to get on with it, and never really suffered from nerves. But I was still a little superstitious. I think most runners do stick to a routine partly out of superstition. The night before a race I would always have my number pinned onto my vest. I did believe that wearing gloves would slow you down but I didn't believe I had a lucky pair of spikes or runners.

I'd been drug tested dozens and dozens of times over the years and I never once worried about testing positive for anything. I was very, very careful from the very beginning about what I should and shouldn't take. I would not try any medicine or cold medicine without checking it first, especially any vitamin or mineral supplement I might have heard about. So all through my career I more or less took the same thing. I took an iron supplement every day, took Vivioptal, a multi-vitamin, Rubex which is purely Vitamin C and cod-liver oil. That was it.

For a long while though I never had any real reason to believe that drug use was a problem in athletics, and least of all Irish athletics. Then Cathal Lombard arrived on the scene.

Lombard was a half-decent club runner in Cork. He'd run well for his club, Leevale, in the National cross-country and on the track, but he'd never won a national title.

In the summer of 2003 he started making some big breakthroughs. He ran

28:05.22 for 10,000 metres and an even more impressive 13:19.22 for 5,000 metres, both of which were apparently big improvements on his previous bests.

Then at the start of May 2004 I heard that Lombard had run 27:33.53 for 10,000 metres at a race in California. That was another massive breakthrough, 13 seconds better than Mark Carroll's Irish record and 15 seconds quicker than John Treacy ever ran.

At that stage a few people were saying that Lombard was on something, that he couldn't be running those times. I still didn't really know what to make of it and given that I had never met him I probably gave him the benefit of the doubt. To be honest I didn't think about it too much given that I was concentrating very much on my own thing.

Towards the end of July I was just finishing a training session in the Phoenix Park, and about to head home, when I spotted Pierce O'Callaghan running towards me. Pierce was a former international walker and was now working with the national governing body, Athletics Ireland.

Did you hear the news, he asked, with a look of real shock and disappointment. Cathal Lombard has been caught, he said. He was taking EPO.

I was simply stunned, and my immediate thought was that Lombard had betrayed both the country and the athletics community.

It took me a few hours to get over the shock, and after that I was just angry at what he had done.

Not long afterwards Lombard issued a statement in which he admitted taking EPO in an effort to reach the top, and had the nerve to suggest that all athletes needed to take it if they truly wanted to mix it with the very best.

I think he made a huge mistake, a stupid mistake, and totally underestimated the consequences. The main reason he was caught was because the Irish Sports Council were very suspicious about his sudden rate of improvement and tested him out of competition on several occasions. Eventually they got lucky and revealed him for the cheat that he was.

Still, I was really hurt to hear him say you can't make it in athletics any more unless you take drugs.

To me that sounded like an ego thing, and that he couldn't handle the fact that he wasn't going to make it without drugs.

The worst part of it was the damage Lombard did to Irish athletics. He was suggesting that a lot of athletes were on the stuff, and of course some people were going to think that meant the other Irish athletes.

His timing couldn't have been any worse either as it all broke just before the Athens Olympics. And I really think he got away with saying that too easy. I don't think he was lambasted nearly enough. He should have paid a higher price than just a two-year suspension.

It took me a while to get over the Lombard scandal. I was really hurt to hear him say you can't make it in athletics any more unless you take drugs. If I had felt that way starting out I don't think I would have got nearly as far as I did. To hear Lombard say no one was going to make it in Ireland without taking drugs was like a slap in the face of all I'd ever done.

I do believe that you need to be 100-per-cent committed to make it in any sport. I think that if I did have any real distractions outside running, such as a love of going out on a Friday night, I would never have made it to the very top. I think the package has to be complete – there can't be any missing parts – in terms of dedication, talent, commitment and hard work.

But as a sport running can operate on so many different levels – from the casual jogger to the elite marathon runner. I would never claim to know everything about running. I think I do know what worked for me, and what didn't, but I don't think anyone can stand up and say they have the recipe for successful running, whether that means winning an Olympic gold medal or just breaking three hours for the marathon.

A lot of different ingredients go into successful running, but those ingredients need to be carefully measured to suit the individual. What works for some athletes may not work for others, and that's why I'd be mindful about giving specific advice or even recommendations to anyone looking to achieve some sort of success in running.

What I can do is look back over my career and detail what helped me achieve the success that I did. It would be foolish for anyone to just copy that, but it's possible that some of the things I did and learnt over the years can help expand the overall understanding of running. But I've always believed that one of the best things about running is its simplicity. That's why I don't think it's a bad idea to give a few simple pieces of advice, which may or may not make running an even more enjoyable part of your life.

Get Started.

There's something about the first week in September that reminds me of starting into another season of running. It's almost like that feeling of going back to school. Instead of digging out the old school uniform, I'd be digging out all my old running gear. It was just like starting another term, feeling a littler older and wiser and full of enthusiasm.

The start of a new term for me was always the start of another cross-country season, and for me that training always started the first week in September. But running is definitely not something that needs to be broken down into a term, or even a season. Running can begin and end at any time of the year. It just happened that my season always began in September, but there's no reason why that season can't begin in January or June or December.

The main reason I say that is because there are no strict rules like that in running. In fact there are very few rules at all. There is no such thing as the running textbook, where you can learn all you need to know about the how, where and when of running. I think it's the same in all sports. There are so many different ways of approaching the training and the preparation and the competition that sometimes the more you know the more confusing it can get.

Unlike starting into a new school term, I never really had much of a break starting into a new season of training. I can look back now and say that was wrong. I never took anything more than a few days of complete rest, when I should have been taking a couple of weeks at least.

That's something I would say to any aspiring athlete, and the same to any seasoned athlete. Make sure you take a complete break from running for between two and three weeks. And that means starting fresh. It's probably a good idea to do something totally different. Like swimming a few times a week, or going cycling. But make sure you get you mind off running.

My feeling was I had to run at least a few miles every day. But now I think there should be a period each year where you shouldn't even think about tying up the laces of your running shoes. It's as much a mental thing as a physical thing. I found out over the years that a lot of the Kenyan and Ethiopian runners take a long break at the end of the year. They even like to go away and get fat, if such a thing is possible. All that means you are really ready to get back into the training, both physically and mentally.

September though was always the time of year when I got back into the regular training routine. For the first few weeks I would concentrate on building mileage, and straight away I would be running seven days a week. Now I would recommend even the most elite athletes to take a day off during that period, or even base their training on an eight-day week, and make the ninth day one of compete rest.

I believe the body needs a full day's rest like that, where you do no running at all. That's the advice that you'll get from most coaches now and I think it's right.

When I was starting back, for the first week or so I would run at least six miles a day, or at least 40 minutes. I think anything less than that is just not worth your while. And I would do that twice a day, say 40 minutes in the morning and another 40 minutes in the evening.

From the first week I would also start straight back into the bounding exercises. So typically in my first week back, starting on the Monday, I would run 40 minutes in the morning and then in the evening do a 20-minute warm-up, following by a bounding session, and then a 20-minute cool-down.

On the Tuesday I would take in a steady run, something just off a tempo run. Usually my tempo runs would be done at a heart rate of about 165 beats per minute, but this run would be at about 150-155. I'd call that a half-tempo run. And I'd do two of them a week, repeating it on the Saturday. On the Wednesday I would do just one 60-minute run. Thursday would be the 40 minutes in the morning and the evening with strides. On the Friday I would normally repeat what I'd done on Monday, and maybe add a few strides afterwards. On the Sunday I'd do another 70-80 minute run with strides.

So I wouldn't be slow at all in easing my way back into the training. Some athletes feel they need to do a few weeks of slow mileage and just steady distance running, but I would always do something more testing from the very start. Still, those runs would always be comfortable.

Get Fitter

I would be back doing my 70 or 80 miles a week more or less from the very start. The only thing that really changed over the course of the season was the intensity, especially when it came to the tempo run. The bounding sessions also increased along the way. When I was starting off it might be only 10 repetitions, but it would build up to 30 repetitions as the weeks passed.

I would also introduce more specific sessions along the way, starting with a hill session. They would usually begin in October. You can't start doing those hill sessions until you have built up a good base. The other big change was the introduction of a track session. That would nearly always start the week before Christmas and invariably meant doing six times 1,000 metres.

Most athletes that run cross-country would be thinking about racing in November, which in Ireland usually meant the Intercounties championships. But they wouldn't want to peak for a race like that either, so they wouldn't be easing down too much in the level of training. For an early race like that it's only important to ease down in training the week before. It's certainly not a good idea to go in having done a hard hill session two or three days before, but neither is it a good idea to back off too much.

I got into the habit of doing a race in Sweden every October, which was a mix between a cross-country race and a trail run. It was about eight miles long and I always found that helped ease me back into racing mode. A 10-kilometre road race could probably have the same effect, as the body does need to get used to racing again, no matter how fit you might feel.

I would treat a race like that as a training run, and something that would break up the routine so it didn't get too boring. I think every athlete needs something like that to look forward to.

Then in the first week of November I would do a low-key cross-country race in Belgium, which again was used as part of the training more than a test of my racing ability at that stage of the season. I would ease down a little bit for that one and do very little running in the two days before.

That got me into a routine where I would do a three-week training block and then ease down in the fourth week in preparation for a race. But immediately after the race I'd go back into another hard week's training. Come the end of November then I would be ready to start racing for real, say at the Inter-counties or one of the grand prix cross country races.

I never resorted to any specific weight-training programme to build strength, even in the build-up to a new season, and I still don't think it's necessary for long-distance running. Strengthening the abdominal muscles is very important.

But when your posture is correct all the time you are working your abdominal muscles. The best way to develop a muscle is by the action you are using. When you run with the correct mechanics you are developing your running muscles and keeping them strong – something I learned from studying Chi running.

It would be a good idea to do some weights to keep your upper body strength.

Get Racing

It's at the racing stage of the season that the more specific elements of running begin to take on greater importance, such as what to eat, and how to spend the hours before getting to the start line. Once again I can only talk about what works for me, but I do know a lot of runners are unsure about what they should be eating in the days or hours before a race. It's a question I've been asked over and over again, and I usually end up telling people just to eat what they are used to eating and not to make any drastic changes.

I would always be aware of what I was eating in the two or three days before a race, and especially in the 24 hours before the race. The first thing to take care of is hydration – make sure to take in plenty of water in the day leading up to the race.

If the race involves some sort of travelling either the day before or the morning of then a bottle of water is an obvious requirement, just something to sip for the duration of the journey, especially if the journey involves a flight.

I got into the routine of taking Dioralite after any long trip or flight. It's designed for infants that have diarrhoea, but the salts and other minerals in it make for an ideal way of ensuring proper hydration after a long journey by plane or car. After a flight I would always mix Dioralite with 200ml of water. I found it very good, and if I was staying in a warm hotel I would take another one the morning after. Most of the commercial sports drinks on the market now will do the job but I didn't have as many to choose from when I was competing in the earlier days.

The most popular pre-race meal for any athlete is pasta, and that was one of my favourites too. But some people make the mistake of eating too much, which can turn out to be as bad as too little. The other mistake is to eat something you're not used to, which can be tempting if you're in a foreign country. Sometimes I'd be in an athletes' hotel before a race and they'd have an array of food put on for us, but I wouldn't touch anything I wasn't used to. I would stick to the simple things like pasta and bread, washed down with plenty of water. I'd even be careful about what kind of sauces they'd put on the pasta, and sometimes I'd end up eating it plain.

There is still that old-fashioned idea of having a good steak the night before a race. It might work for some people, but a meal like that does take a long time to digest, maybe as long as 48 hours. So I avoided all meats in the day or two before a race. I'd make sure I'd get my share earlier in the week, right up to the Thursday or Friday, but never on the day before the race.

As for heavy desserts and things like that I think most athletes know where to draw the line. What I would do was take a banana or two back to my room. I found they helped me sleep, and if I woke up during the night I'd have a couple of bites of a banana. That usually sent me straight back to sleep.

It's also very important to watch what you eat the morning of a race. My tried and trusted breakfast was porridge, which I happened to love as a young-ster and always enjoyed the morning of a race. It reached the stage where I would always bring a bag of my own porridge oats no matter where I was going. I would give that to the hotel staff the night before and ask them to cook it up for me in the morning. I did that right through my career and I know a few of the other runners would look at me and wonder what I was up to. But that's what I liked and that's what I wanted on the morning of a race. A bowl of porridge and a few slices of bread were always enough for me.

Get Ready

It's very important to be careful about the amount of time you leave between eating and racing. Leave it too late and it won't be digested properly, but eat too soon and you may feel hungry. I always wanted to finish eating three and a half hours before my race. I would have nothing after that except water. If the race wasn't off until three in the afternoon I would get up and have a little bit of fruit, and then have breakfast about 11.30.

I know it amazes some people when I say I never drank tea or coffee. I don't think drinking tea or coffee before a race does you any harm, as long as it's in moderation. I know that tea and coffee do dehydrate you and that's the last thing you want going into a race. But if you like the taste of one or the other and feel you can't survive without it, there's no reason not to have a cup.

Finding the right level of hydration is a happy medium, and something to work on. But no one wants to be thirsty going into a race. It's possible to drink too much water, which can lead to a stitch or stomach cramp, not to mention running to the toilet every five minutes. That's not a good idea either. Sipping on a small bottle in the hours leading up to the race is the proper thing to do.

When it came to running marathons I still stuck to that same eating routine. I would eat more in the days beforehand, but breakfast was always the same. The London marathon started at 9.00 so that meant getting up at 5.30 for the porridge. I'd just lie in bed after that and wait for the time to pass.

The drinks during the marathon itself were crucial. I used to use Maxim, which was a pure carbohydrate drink. I'd take in 200ml every 5 kilometres. It wasn't that much to drink but it definitely kept the carbohydrates topped up.

After a race some athletes have a hard time eating, especially if they've run very hard. It is important to take something in as soon as possible, in the first 20 minutes preferably. I would also have a full carbohydrate drink as soon as possible.

I know now it's important to take in some protein as soon as possible as well, even after a hard training session. But what I would always look forward to after a hard race was a big plate of potatoes. If I was going home afterwards my mother would always have a big pot of potatoes on the boil waiting for me, and the bigger the potatoes the better.

I remember the first time I was served these tiny little potatoes, the kind you get in the so-called posh restaurants. My father couldn't believe anyone would eat them. He'd say that years ago we wouldn't have even thrown them to the pigs. I remember picking potatoes at home and we would always leave the little ones like that in the ground. As much as I love potatoes I would never eat those things. What you want is a big, floury potato, with a nice lump of butter. And throw away the skin.

I'm definitely not the best person to give advice on drinking alcohol before or after a race because I never once did it. Some people need a beer or two to relax after a race and I can't imagine that does them any harm. I don't even know if any athletes I ran against ever liked a drink after a race because I was always gone off to bed when it came to that stage of the night. Before a race I would be in bed at 9.30-10.00, happily reading a book. Two nights before is the most important night of all, so to have sleep problems the night before a race is not the end of the world.

Get it Right

I would start warming up maybe an hour to 45 minutes before a race, running somewhere between 15 and 20 minutes. I used to do a fair amount of stretching as well but I'm not so sure now if all that was necessary. I know from chi running there are some body-loosening exercise that are much better at warming up the joints, and that's what I do now even before a run. So I wouldn't recommend anyone does too much stretching before a race. The muscles won't be warm enough and you could end up straining or pulling a muscle.

After the warm-up though I would always do five or six long strides to get the heart rate up. It would take me a while to get going, so I would get the strides going at the same pace as I would start out the race, in order to practise going from the gun.

If everything has gone to plan in the days and hours before a race then the body should respond once the starting gun is fired. Joe Doonan was great at helping me reach my peak, and I never had any problems peaking for a major race.

When it came to say the World Cross Country I would always cut back substantially on the training, and that made sure I was well tapered. For the last 10 days I would do nothing too strenuous. Joe used to say this was my holiday period, and it was. I'd have a lot of time on my hands because I wasn't doing nearly as much running as usual.

There is no such thing as the perfect taper, but there has to be a significant reduction in the training if the body wants to produce that one big performance that you have been training for. My tapering was always quite strict before a major race, particularly cross country and the marathon. But I never felt like I was fully rested for the track races perhaps because at that stage of the year I was getting tired and stale. Any time I did a track session it always felt difficult.

If that race was on the Sunday, which it usually was, I'd do a short hill session on the Tuesday, and no more than five repetitions. During the hard training I'd do 10 repetitions.

Even my warm-ups and cool-downs were cut right back. So I would always go into a major race feeling fresh.

A lot of runners make the mistake of training hard in the days before a race, and I have made that mistake a few times myself on the track. But I always went into the cross-country races that mattered feeling fresh, and the only way you can do that is by easing right down in the training in the week or 10 days before.

It was the same when it came to the track. My last track session was about a week before, and instead of doing six times 1,000 metres, I would do only three. But maybe a little faster, around two minutes 55 seconds instead of three minutes. In the days immediately before the race I would do nothing more than a 25 or 30-minute run.

The tapering for a marathon was even more extreme in that I would do very little running in the week beforehand. My last long run, 20 miles, was always three weeks before the race, because there is no benefit at all in doing it any later than that.

It's probably worth detailing that marathon taper because it always worked for me.

On the Sunday before I would do a one-hour run at marathon pace, and that always felt easy. That was a full week before. On the Monday I would do an easy 40-minute run. On the Tuesday I'd do a short warm-up and then run three by seven minutes at marathon pace.

That was still only about 21 minutes of work, and I would do it somewhere flat, such as a golf course. On the Wednesday and Thursday I'd just do another 40-minute run. On the Friday before the race I would do 15 minutes easy, then 15 minutes at marathon pace, then another 15 minutes easy.

That was a complete taper in the training compared to the miles I would have been doing in the weeks before. That's essential in marathon running, because there's just no way anyone should go into a marathon feeling tired from training.

Get There

It's almost impossible to give general advice on marathon training because obviously running 26.2 miles can present an entirely different challenge to one person from what it would present to another. If someone has been running for a few years there's no reason why they can't attempt a marathon within a few months, but it's a different story if someone is starting from scratch.

How long does it take to prepare for a marathon? That's another question I've been asked lots of times. Again it's very hard to give advice in that situation, but generally it means starting to prepare seriously about four months in advance. That would be for someone who's done a fair amount of running before, and possibly finished a marathon or two. For someone starting out completely form scratch, however, at least six or seven months, and more likely a year, would be necessary.

There are a lot of things that need to be taken into account when someone is starting into marathon training. The most important thing is to have a bit of a base. Running three or four times a week will help establish that. Marathon training is definitely not something you want to rush. Unlike studying for an exam, there is no such thing as a crash course in marathon running, or even any way of cramming the training.

When it comes to mile 24 or 25 there's no place to hide, and any lack of proper preparation will quickly be revealed. But for anyone who has built up a reasonable base of running, four months – or 16 weeks – should be long enough to fine-tune the preparations.

There are a few common pitfalls in marathon training, the first of which is trying to do too much too soon. It's a bad idea to try running too far in the first week or so, and anybody who feels they need to be running 10 or 15 miles every day from the beginning will soon run into problems. Even with a good base it's better to build up gradually, making sure not to jump from running 40 miles a week to 80 miles a week. Weekly mileage should not be increased by more than 10% per week.

The temptation is always there to run more miles, and one of the enduring misconceptions about marathon training is that the more miles that are run in a week the better the result. It's not quite that simple. First of all the body won't

recover the way it needs to between training sessions, and there's a strong possibility of overdoing it, resulting in burnout or injury.

I never ran more than 110 miles a week, even when I was in the most intense
periods of marathon training. I know a lot of elite runners, men and women,
push their mileage a lot higher than that, maybe as high as 130 or 140 miles a
week. That might work for some, but it's definitely too high for most people. But
I never went any higher than 110, even when I was training at altitude.

I found that amount manageable and actually quite enjoyable. When I first
moved up to the marathon training in the summer of 1997 I found the intensity wasn't quite as demanding as it was on the track or even cross-country.
Marathon training is a lot more about quantity than quality, but it is still important to get the balance right. Run too many miles and the overall quality will
drop, but run too few miles and you won't get the quantity you need.

I was always very comfortable in the marathon-training zone in terms of
mileage and the heart rate I needed to hit on my harder sessions. I sometimes
felt I could run on and on at that pace without ever stopping. It was different
on the track, where one hard injection of pace could kill my race. You never got
that same injection in the marathon, and that's one reason why I was able to
handle the distance so well.

One of my favourite marathon sessions was five times 12 minutes at
marathon pace. I would build up to that, starting with five times six minutes,
then seven minutes, and so on up. Some people would dread a session like that,
but once I got into the zone I found it very easy and very enjoyable. It felt so
comfortable that I would often feel better at the end of the session than I did
at the start.

Get Better

Preparing to run 26.2 miles at speed is a little complicated, but it's certainly not
rocket science. One of the first things I was told about on my visits to the
human-performance laboratory in Trinity College was the use of a heart-rate
monitor. I more or less used the monitor from the very beginning. Some people
find them uncomfortable, but I got used to them from the start, and it became
a part of me whenever the training got serious.

I don't think any elite runner can operate without a heart-rate monitor. If anyone is serious about running a fast marathon time then they'll need to get the necessary physiological testing to assess what state of fitness they are at, and that will allow them use their heart-rate as an indication of their training. The only way they can do that accurately is with a heart-rate monitor.

Without a heart-rate monitor it's going to be very difficult to assess improvements, and whether or not the heart-rate is being worked on the way it needs to be. The body will always give you a fair idea of how hard or how easy you're working, but if you want to be truly professional about it then the heart-rate monitor is essential.

Most days I would work off the heart rate, making sure the easy days stayed easy, and the hard days were as hard as they needed to be. Sometimes I would find it hard on my tempo runs to get my heart rate up to the level I needed to. If I wasn't getting that information from the heart-rate monitor then I wouldn't have been pushing myself as hard and obviously wouldn't have made the kind of progression in training that I needed to.

There were other days when I wanted to run somewhere between the two. My heart rate for tempo runs was 165 beats per minute, and my easy run was 135, but I used to do some in-between runs of 155. On days like that I would find myself hitting 160 quite easy, so it was important to back off a little in that situation. Essentially the heart-rate monitor served two purposes: it made sure I was training hard enough when I needed to, and it helped me run easy enough when I needed to, so that I didn't overtrain.

It takes a little bit of work to establish the zones you'll want to be working at, but it's worth the effort. I don't know of many elite runners that get away without using a heart-rate monitor, because it is going to be very difficult to make improvements unless you know the heart is being worked the way it needs to. My advice for anyone thinking of running a marathon in the elite bracket is to get a monitor. You won't succeed without one.

For most levels of marathon running, however, steady training is the only secret. That's not to say you can't use a little bit of sports science. From my earliest days as a competitive runner I would always check my pulse first thing in the morning. My own resting pulse was 38 beats per minute. If it was a few beats above normal then it usually meant I was overtraining a little bit, or possibly carrying a little virus.

To be honest I would plough on with it more often than not, but I think all runners could benefit from a regular check of their own pulse. Obviously if it was sky high, racing into the 50s, I would take a rest day or two, but if it's only three or four beats above normal it's probably still okay to train.

Get Winning

The first piece of advice I would give to any runner lining up for a race is not to go off too fast. Careful pacing is the key to a good race, no matter what the distance. And unless it's the 100 metres, most races require some careful pacing. Going off too hard will almost certainly result in negative consequences, no matter how fit the athlete is. The body will go into oxygen debt if put under too much strain too soon, and it will have a hard time recovering.

For those thinking of winning a race, strategy plays an equally important role as pacing. At some stage it means making a break and injecting what is hoped will be a winning surge. My belief is that it should be done gradually. I won a lot of cross-country races by adopting that strategy, say moving up beside the leaders and running on their shoulders for a while before making my move. It's a good idea to check out their breathing or their facial expressions to get some idea of how they're feeling.

But when the break is made it will have to be decisive. Don't half do it, or don't pretend to do it. I would always make one hard surge and wouldn't stop until I was sure I was away from everyone else. It doesn't mean sprinting flat out, but it does mean lengthening the stride and working harder than at any other stage in the race. My sprint finish wasn't the best in the world and that meant I would usually make that surge quite a ways out from the finish, certainly before the last mile. Some athletes can afford to leave it until the last 100 metres, but either way it has to be controlled, because you don't want to mess it up.

I found that by doing 1,000-metre repeats on the track during the cross-country season I always had the leg speed I needed to make the surges I needed to, and to hold the surge until I got away.

Still, I did end up in quite a few sprint finishes over the years, starting with the World Cross Country in Boston in 1992, when Lynn Jennings beat me to the line. When I found myself in a similar situation at the European Cross

Country in 1994 I realised that the will to win is sometimes as important as your ability to sprint. I was battling for the line with Julia Vaquero of Spain, but I think I wanted to win it more than her. So I give her a little elbow to make sure she knew that. But you have to go for it like that and think of nothing else except winning.

Tactics play an even greater role in track races. The only way to win on the track is to prepare to win. The main difference in my training when it came to the track was an increase in the number of repetitions. In the earlier days I started out doing repeat 400 metres, like most people do. It was only later that I developed the individually tailored sessions. One of those was to do run 4,000 metres by two, and then 1,000 metres by two. The 4,000-metre interval was broken down into 400 metres fast and 400 metres steady. Then 300 metres fast and 300 metres steady. Overall that was 10,000-metres worth of session, and it was hard going.

There's no doubt that it is easier to overtrain on the track, simply because of the intensity of the sessions. Part of my problem was that I always had a hard cross-country season behind me, and looking back now I know that's one of the main reasons why my track races weren't as successful as they could have been.

It's a long time from September until the following July, so I would strongly recommend anyone who runs both seasons with any sort of intensity to take a good break in between. I never did, and I always found myself getting more and more tired as the track season wore on. I'd usually be flying at the beginning but fatigue would eventually set in.

I don't think anyone ran the cross-country season as intensely as I did and then repeated the form on the track. It just wasn't physically possible. You find even the Kenyans and the Ethiopians usually end up missing a cross-country season every odd year or so and gearing just towards the track.

Get Healthy

The first course of action with any injury is rest. A day or two off won't break a season, but it will give a better idea of how serious the problem might be. Ice is also a good treatment, especially in the first 48 hours.

Now more than ever I believe running injuries are all connected to running mechanics. If you're getting a pain in your knee or shins or sole, it is because your feet are landing out in front of you and you are breaking with every stride causing terrible pressure on your knees.

If your calves are tight you're probably pushing off your feet, instead of lifting them. And if the hamstring is tight you are grabbing with every stride overworking your hamstring. What you do to prevent this is tilt or lean your posture forward and allow gravity to do the work for you and give your hamstrings a break. So prevention is far better than cure. It's not running that injures you but the way your run.

I endured some really terrible times with injury, and I hate to see any athlete not being able to run because of injury. There were two times in my life when I said to myself that I never wanted to run again, and on both occasions it was because of injury. I had an operation on my knee after the Amsterdam marathon on 1998, and when I woke up after the anaesthetic I was so horribly sick that I just wanted to die. I couldn't believe running had brought this about, and I didn't want anything more to do with it.

The other time was before the Sydney Olympics, when I had an MRI scan on my back. I was lying there in this tunnel for about 45 minutes, and all I could hear was this clicking noise. I couldn't move any part of my body, and that sort of thing would kill my enthusiasm. I know so many people go through illnesses an awful lot worse than that, but those things turned me so far off running.

Sometimes if you can just relax about the injury it will heal quicker. An injury can also be a warning sign that you are overdoing the training, and once you ease back a little bit it goes away. Sometimes when athletes are injured they go rushing off to the swimming pool or out on the bike in case they lose any fitness, when in fact the injury was the body's way of telling them to slow down and take a breather. So that's something to be aware of too.

Even the most successful of runners will sometimes have a hard time keeping up the enthusiasm for hard training, especially if they're at it year after year. So it's a good idea to ease off every now and then.

I don't believe running shoes or even running surfaces contribute to injuries. Whatever shoe feels comfortable is probably a good one. Shoes are expensive now, but a simple, neutral shoe is usually best. I stay away from something with a big heel support or too much cushioning, because a lot of shoes these days actually weaken the foot. I think a light shoe is always better than a heavy shoe.

I would change my shoes every 500 miles of so, but you know yourself when you need a new pair.

People who are forced to run on the roads all the time need to take special care about their running style. It's important that they're not pounding the roads, because that does cause more stress on the body than running on grass. But again I would say that if you run with the correct mechanics, you will not hurt yourself.

Get Advice

I think any athlete will tell you it's almost impossible to get the best out of yourself in training and racing without a coach. And I would definitely agree. You need somebody there to direct you. Otherwise there will always be the temptation to take the easy option or over train.

It's good to have training partners as well. I did almost all my training alone. Now I feel it's much easier to have someone train with you and it passes the time much quicker.

But a coach will also help develop a plan and make sure it's properly followed. Just copying some other athlete's training sessions is not a good idea. Every runner needs to be confident in their own training plan, rather than blindly copying what other people are doing. I know a lot of runners are fascinated by what others do in training, but it's not a good idea to do adopt a particular training regime just because somebody else is doing it.

All athletes are different, even in terms of when they like to run. I can usually run 50 or 60 minutes after getting out of bed in the morning. But when it comes to the harder sessions or longer runs statistics show that the best time to do a hard session is between 4.00pm and 6.00pm. Your body gets the best benefit at this time. But either way it's best to work around what suits the daily schedule, because I know some people don't feel like running first thing in the morning.

It's also a good idea to run a few fast strides at the end or in the middle of some runs, just to get the legs used to turning over that bit quicker. It might be just 10 or 15 seconds faster per mile than usual. It's also a good idea to run a few fast strides at the end or in the middle of some runs just to get the legs used to turning over that bit faster. There's no harm in playing around with a little bit of speed like that.

Whatever the level of running, whether it's 20 minutes after work or two hours on a Sunday morning, the most important thing of all is to enjoy it. If running ever becomes a chore then something has gone wrong. That's not to say running is always going to be easy. Success in running, like in any other walk of life, involves hard work over a long period of time. But the rewards can be great, and lasting. Running can create a feeling of wellbeing second to none. I don't think I need to tell anyone that.

ENDS